ESSENTIAL SKILLS IN MATHS

BOOK 2

Nelson

Graham Newman and Ron Bull

D1354854

35776A

First published in 1996 by:
Thomas Nelson and Sons Ltd

Reprinted in 2001 by:
Nelson Thornes Ltd
Delta Place
27 Bath Road
CHELTENHAM
GL53 7TH
United Kingdom

03 04 05 06 / 19 18 17 16 15 14 13 12

A catalogue record for this book is available from the British Library

ISBN 0 17 431441 8

Printed and bound in China by L.Rex

Contents

Number

1/ MENTAL ARITHMETIC: ADDING AND SUBTRACTING TWO 2-DIGIT NUMBERS WITHOUT A CALCULATOR

When working with a number that is almost a 'round number', for example 10, 20 or 30, the calculation can be made easier by using the round number and then adjusting the answer at the end.

EXAMPLE

▶ 35 + 19

19 is nearly 20:   35 + 20 = 55

but 20 was used instead of 19:   55 – 1 = 54

EXAMPLE

▶ 87 – 48

48 is nearly 50:   87 – 50 = 37

50 was taken away instead of 48, give 2 back: 37 + 2 = 39

Another method for solving additions and subtractions in your head is to split one of the numbers into tens and units and do the calculation in two easy parts.

EXAMPLE

▶ 37 + 24

24 is 20 + 4:   4 + 37 = 41

Now add the 20:   41 + 20 = 61

EXAMPLE

▶ 54 – 36

Take away 6:   54 – 6 = 48

Take away 30:   48 – 30 = 18

Exercise 1A

Do these calculations in your head; do *not* use a calculator.

1 36 + 35	**2** 66 – 11	**3** 52 + 31	**4** 79 – 29	**5** 76 + 13
6 88 – 12	**7** 68 + 21	**8** 26 + 47	**9** 67 – 25	**10** 16 + 49
11 54 + 34	**12** 41 + 58	**13** 78 + 18	**14** 59 – 15	**15** 55 – 48
16 96 – 22	**17** 17 + 24	**18** 32 + 56	**19** 44 – 23	**20** 14 + 38
21 65 – 43	**22** 28 + 77	**23** 39 + 69	**24** 45 + 57	**25** 64 – 27
26 33 + 63	**27** 53 – 46	**28** 37 + 89	**29** 84 – 19	**30** 74 – 42

Exercise 1B

Do these calculations in your head; do *not* use a calculator.

1 21 + 74	**2** 44 – 32	**3** 52 – 38	**4** 31 + 46	**5** 14 + 89
6 58 – 33	**7** 79 – 24	**8** 11 + 85	**9** 56 + 28	**10** 55 – 39

11 76 − 17	**12** 19 + 78	**13** 57 − 15	**14** 18 + 65	**15** 42 + 53
16 64 − 22	**17** 13 + 88	**18** 47 − 26	**19** 51 − 23	**20** 36 + 59
21 63 − 25	**22** 12 + 83	**23** 94 − 16	**24** 29 + 67	**25** 48 + 54
26 77 − 35	**27** 61 − 43	**28** 49 + 66	**29** 68 − 37	**30** 75 + 45

2/ ADDING AND SUBTRACTING TWO 3-DIGIT NUMBERS WITHOUT A CALCULATOR

Exercise 2A

1 362 + 235	**2** 432 + 153	**3** 735 − 621	**4** 612 − 109	**5** 453 + 234
6 331 + 522	**7** 217 + 254	**8** 632 − 419	**9** 544 − 354	**10** 266 − 169
11 109 + 545	**12** 580 + 227	**13** 642 − 316	**14** 740 − 243	**15** 236 + 163
16 956 − 887	**17** 278 + 119	**18** 553 − 385	**19** 430 − 223	**20** 265 + 409
21 418 − 156	**22** 809 − 656	**23** 337 + 394	**24** 805 − 479	**25** 612 + 384
26 555 − 465	**27** 406 − 199	**28** 388 + 425	**29** 727 − 218	**30** 645 + 178

Exercise 2B

1 324 + 243	**2** 512 + 375	**3** 236 + 332	**4** 575 − 304	**5** 614 − 203
6 581 − 425	**7** 837 + 116	**8** 580 + 329	**9** 624 − 555	**10** 409 − 218
11 689 − 607	**12** 307 + 485	**13** 418 + 289	**14** 561 − 244	**15** 173 + 346
16 664 − 482	**17** 518 + 305	**18** 682 − 477	**19** 705 − 318	**20** 911 − 429
21 368 + 554	**22** 422 + 361	**23** 309 − 199	**24** 427 + 573	**25** 731 − 439
26 844 − 667	**27** 621 − 239	**28** 588 + 186	**29** 379 + 585	**30** 274 + 597

3/ ADDING AND SUBTRACTING SEVERAL 1-DIGIT NUMBERS WITHOUT A CALCULATOR

Exercise 3A

1 2 + 5 + 6 + 8	**2** 4 + 6 + 8 + 2	**3** 3 + 1 + 6 + 4	**4** 5 + 8 + 2 + 6
5 3 + 5 + 6 + 4	**6** 9 + 2 + 4 + 3	**7** 4 + 7 + 3 + 8	**8** 7 + 6 + 2 + 4
9 6 + 5 + 3 + 8	**10** 4 + 8 + 2 + 7	**11** 2 + 5 + 7 − 8	**12** 4 + 5 − 8 + 5
13 8 + 0 − 5 + 2	**14** 6 + 7 − 3 + 4	**15** 2 + 6 + 7 − 9	**16** 8 − 9 + 3 − 1
17 5 + 7 − 6 + 2	**18** 3 − 6 + 4 + 5	**19** 1 + 8 + 9 − 7	**20** 6 + 4 + 4 − 5 + 4
21 2 + 5 + 0 + 8 − 2	**22** 1 − 9 + 7 + 3 + 3	**23** 4 − 2 + 7 − 8 + 6	
24 2 + 3 + 8 + 4 + 7 − 5	**25** 3 + 5 + 7 + 9 − 6 − 2	**26** 4 + 5 + 3 + 0 + 4 + 6	
27 9 − 2 − 3 − 1 + 6 − 2	**28** 2 + 3 + 2 + 5 + 6 + 4 + 2	**29** 3 + 4 − 5 − 1 + 3 − 5 + 7	
30 5 + 7 − 6 − 9 + 8 + 6 + 4			

Exercise 3B

1 2 + 6 + 4 + 3	**2** 5 + 4 + 3 + 6	**3** 1 + 6 + 8 + 2	**4** 3 + 5 + 6 + 2
5 6 + 7 + 2 + 4	**6** 2 + 4 + 6 + 3	**7** 5 + 4 + 1 + 8	**8** 6 + 4 + 8 + 2
9 8 + 3 + 7 + 4	**10** 5 + 8 + 6 + 2	**11** 4 + 6 + 5 - 3	**12** 5 + 7 - 4 + 3
13 2 + 9 + 6 - 5	**14** 8 - 6 + 2 + 7	**15** 6 + 5 - 7 + 4	**16** 3 - 8 + 2 + 6
17 5 - 6 + 2 + 8 + 5	**18** 2 + 3 + 8 + 5 - 9	**19** 4 - 8 - 3 + 5 + 6	**20** 9 + 8 + 9 - 7 - 6
21 2 + 5 + 6 - 3 + 8 - 4	**22** 6 + 4 - 2 - 3 - 1 + 8	**23** 5 - 7 - 8 + 6 + 4 + 5	
24 1 + 2 + 6 + 4 + 3 + 7 + 2	**25** 2 + 5 - 3 + 4 + 8 + 2 + 4	**26** 3 + 5 - 4 - 6 + 9 - 3 + 4	
27 5 + 5 + 6 + 4 - 9 - 9 + 8	**28** 6 - 9 - 8 - 7 + 6 + 6 + 5 + 4	**29** 7 + 5 - 6 - 3 + 2 + 4 + 6 - 2	
30 3 + 5 + 7 + 9 - 8 - 6 - 4 + 3			

4/ NUMBERS TO WORDS

EXAMPLE

▶ Write 2534 in words.

Two thousand, five hundred and thirty-four

EXAMPLE

▶ Write 523 650 in words.

Five hundred and twenty-three thousand, six hundred and fifty

EXAMPLE

▶ Write 21 009 100 in words.

Twenty-one million, nine thousand, one hundred

Exercise 4A

Write in words.

1 2500	**2** 1863	**3** 9005	**4** 10 005	**5** 11 998
6 91 250	**7** 55 506	**8** 32 025	**9** 74 288	**10** 26 293
11 15 000	**12** 55 055	**13** 87 660	**14** 40 010	**15** 180 309
16 559 000	**17** 999 000	**18** 281 030	**19** 90 054	**20** 750 010
21 3 588 000	**22** 758 860	**23** 21 000 000	**24** 5 500 000	**25** 812 000
26 6 100 008	**27** 80 000 500	**28** 540 000 000	**29** 10 250 000	**30** 26 000 020

Exercise 4B

Write in words.

1 1500	**2** 7934	**3** 2650	**4** 35 690	**5** 14 600
6 86 100	**7** 13 242	**8** 27 200	**9** 50 001	**10** 19 002
11 12 550	**12** 10 567	**13** 65 862	**14** 119 663	**15** 396 500
16 245 000	**17** 330 000	**18** 631 866	**19** 490 000	**20** 950 050

21 1 000 001	**22** 9 100 000	**23** 5 060 005	**24** 7 879 400	**25** 55 000 000
26 14 500 000	**27** 900 000 000	**28** 85 000 000	**29** 40 500 000	**30** 13 000 500

5/ WORDS TO NUMBERS

EXAMPLE
▶ Write two thousand, three hundred and eighteen in number form.

2318

EXAMPLE
▶ Write seven hundred and forty-five thousand, three hundred and fifty-seven in number form.

745 357

EXAMPLE
▶ Write two hundred and three million, five hundred thousand in number form.

203 500 000

Exercise 5A

Write in number form.

1   Five thousand and one
2   One thousand, nine hundred and forty-two
3   Thirty-one thousand
4   Eighty-seven thousand, two hundred
5   Twenty-seven thousand, seven hundred and fifty
6   Twenty thousand and five
7   Eighty-three thousand, two hundred and seventy
8   One hundred thousand, three hundred
9   Two hundred and ninety-nine thousand, nine hundred and ninety
10   Seven hundred and seventy-three thousand and eight
11   Four hundred and thirty-four thousand, six hundred and thirty
12   One hundred and ninety-five thousand, two hundred and ten
13   One hundred and twenty-three thousand, five hundred and twenty
14   Eight hundred and ninety-seven thousand
15   Eight million, five hundred and sixty-one thousand
16   Twenty million
17   Two million, one hundred and fifty thousand
18   Ninety-nine million, nine hundred and ten thousand
19   Six hundred and fifty million
20   One million and eighty-five

Exercise 5B

Write in number form.

1   Nine thousand, five hundred and forty-eight

2	Four thousand, one hundred and thirty-five

2 Four thousand, one hundred and thirty-five
3 Thirty-eight thousand, five hundred
4 Fourteen thousand and two
5 Fifty-three thousand, three hundred and twelve
6 Eighty-two thousand, seven hundred and sixty-seven
7 Fifteen thousand, four hundred and forty-four
8 Forty-nine thousand and seventy
9 Thirty thousand, four hundred and fifty-five
10 Twenty-one thousand and ninety
11 Sixty-one thousand, seven hundred
12 Three hundred and five thousand
13 Four hundred thousand
14 Thirteen thousand, eight hundred and fifty
15 Three hundred and seventy thousand, six hundred and eighty-nine
16 Eleven thousand, five hundred
17 Sixty-seven million, five hundred thousand
18 Six million, eight hundred thousand and thirteen
19 Seven hundred and fifty million
20 One hundred and one million

6/ TABLES: TO 10 × 10

Exercise 6A

1	5×5	**2**	6×3	**3**	4×5	**4**	3×7	**5**	5×3
6	3×6	**7**	2×9	**8**	3×8	**9**	5×4	**10**	3×9
11	4×6	**12**	3×5	**13**	6×4	**14**	5×7	**15**	4×9
16	7×3	**17**	7×10	**18**	2×8	**19**	7×4	**20**	6×5
21	5×10	**22**	4×8	**23**	6×6	**24**	9×3	**25**	7×5
26	8×3	**27**	2×7	**28**	5×9	**29**	6×8	**30**	5×6
31	8×4	**32**	6×7	**33**	5×8	**34**	8×6	**35**	9×5
36	8×7	**37**	6×9	**38**	7×8	**39**	9×6	**40**	8×5
41	7×9	**42**	7×7	**43**	2×6	**44**	9×10	**45**	9×4
46	4×7	**47**	8×9	**48**	7×6	**49**	8×8	**50**	9×7
51	6×5	**52**	4×6	**53**	3×9	**54**	8×3	**55**	7×4
56	5×8	**57**	8×4	**58**	6×7	**59**	3×8	**60**	5×6
61	4×8	**62**	7×5	**63**	5×9	**64**	6×6	**65**	5×4
66	3×7	**67**	5×3	**68**	6×9	**69**	5×10	**70**	5×5
71	3×6	**72**	9×4	**73**	10×6	**74**	7×7	**75**	9×8
76	7×9	**77**	10×7	**78**	8×6	**79**	2×8	**80**	9×5
81	2×7	**82**	4×9	**83**	8×8	**84**	7×6	**85**	6×3
86	8×10	**87**	4×7	**88**	7×8	**89**	2×9	**90**	9×7
91	8×9	**92**	7×3	**93**	9×6	**94**	8×5	**95**	9×3
96	6×8	**97**	5×7	**98**	8×7	**99**	6×4	**100**	9×9

Exercise 6B

1	6×3	**2**	3×5	**3**	4×3	**4**	5×5	**5**	2×6
6	5×4	**7**	7×3	**8**	6×7	**9**	2×5	**10**	4×4
11	8×3	**12**	4×7	**13**	5×9	**14**	8×4	**15**	5×6
16	7×4	**17**	10×3	**18**	3×8	**19**	5×10	**20**	3×7
21	4×5	**22**	9×3	**23**	4×6	**24**	2×8	**25**	4×9
26	6×8	**27**	7×5	**28**	5×3	**29**	6×6	**30**	2×9
31	3×4	**32**	6×4	**33**	8×5	**34**	9×4	**35**	7×8
36	9×8	**37**	6×5	**38**	8×8	**39**	3×6	**40**	7×7
41	8×9	**42**	5×7	**43**	8×4	**44**	8×6	**45**	9×5
46	4×8	**47**	6×9	**48**	9×7	**49**	7×6	**50**	6×10
51	9×8	**52**	7×9	**53**	10×8	**54**	9×6	**55**	3×9
56	8×7	**57**	5×8	**58**	9×4	**59**	6×10	**60**	10×5
61	4×7	**62**	7×3	**63**	5×5	**64**	3×4	**65**	4×5
66	5×3	**67**	6×4	**68**	10×5	**69**	3×7	**70**	6×3
71	5×4	**72**	4×6	**73**	7×5	**74**	4×4	**75**	10×7
76	5×9	**77**	4×8	**78**	5×6	**79**	7×4	**80**	6×9
81	9×6	**82**	8×7	**83**	6×5	**84**	8×3	**85**	6×7
86	4×9	**87**	6×8	**88**	3×9	**89**	8×6	**90**	5×7
91	9×9	**92**	5×8	**93**	7×7	**94**	8×9	**95**	7×8
96	6×6	**97**	7×9	**98**	8×8	**99**	7×6	**100**	9×7

7/ MULTIPLICATION AND DIVISION BY A 1-DIGIT NUMBER WITHOUT A CALCULATOR

Exercise 7A

1	18×2	**2**	37×3	**3**	$52 \div 2$	**4**	36×4	**5**	$24 \div 3$
6	$92 \div 4$	**7**	13×5	**8**	22×8	**9**	28×3	**10**	$76 \div 2$
11	$40 \div 8$	**12**	33×7	**13**	97×2	**14**	26×4	**15**	$80 \div 5$
16	$210 \div 7$	**17**	75×5	**18**	$42 \div 7$	**19**	17×8	**20**	29×2
21	$30 \div 2$	**22**	$60 \div 4$	**23**	78×2	**24**	$54 \div 6$	**25**	$84 \div 7$
26	51×7	**27**	52×8	**28**	$48 \div 8$	**29**	$78 \div 3$	**30**	68×6

Exercise 7B

1	$45 \div 3$	**2**	$32 \div 2$	**3**	27×2	**4**	65×3	**5**	19×5
6	$82 \div 2$	**7**	$28 \div 4$	**8**	$95 \div 5$	**9**	87×2	**10**	47×5
11	14×3	**12**	$88 \div 8$	**13**	$56 \div 7$	**14**	$36 \div 3$	**15**	21×7
16	76×6	**17**	93×5	**18**	89×4	**19**	$64 \div 4$	**20**	$96 \div 8$
21	$90 \div 6$	**22**	$72 \div 9$	**23**	25×3	**24**	41×9	**25**	13×6
26	43×7	**27**	$98 \div 7$	**28**	$65 \div 5$	**29**	94×7	**30**	53×6

Exercise 7C

1	49 × 4	**2**	32 × 7	**3**	125 ÷ 5	**4**	108 ÷ 9	**5**	342 ÷ 3
6	702 ÷ 6	**7**	35 × 2	**8**	92 × 6	**9**	15 × 8	**10**	29 × 9
11	240 ÷ 8	**12**	144 ÷ 9	**13**	180 ÷ 4	**14**	196 ÷ 7	**15**	196 ÷ 4
16	38 × 4	**17**	71 × 9	**18**	39 × 6	**19**	72 × 5	**20**	132 ÷ 6
21	320 ÷ 4	**22**	150 ÷ 6	**23**	69 × 3	**24**	63 × 4	**25**	79 × 8
26	84 × 7	**27**	360 ÷ 9	**28**	140 ÷ 4	**29**	120 ÷ 8	**30**	45 × 8

Exercise 7D

1	81 × 6	**2**	86 × 2	**3**	732 ÷ 4	**4**	720 ÷ 9	**5**	73 × 4
6	77 × 3	**7**	91 × 9	**8**	330 ÷ 6	**9**	62 × 9	**10**	200 ÷ 8
11	195 ÷ 3	**12**	31 × 8	**13**	364 ÷ 7	**14**	48 × 9	**15**	745 ÷ 5
16	67 × 8	**17**	513 ÷ 9	**18**	185 ÷ 5	**19**	74 × 3	**20**	34 × 9
21	819 ÷ 9	**22**	651 ÷ 3	**23**	83 × 5	**24**	85 × 6	**25**	112 ÷ 8
26	115 ÷ 5	**27**	95 × 4	**28**	402 ÷ 6	**29**	137 × 7	**30**	356 × 8

8/ MULTIPLYING AND DIVIDING BY POWERS OF 10

Simple rules

× 10	'add' a zero	× 100	'add' two zeros	× 1000	'add' three zeros
÷ 10	'lose' a zero	÷ 100	'lose' two zeros	÷ 1000	'lose' three zeros

EXAMPLES

▶ 24 × 10 = 24<u>0</u>
32 × 1000 = 32 <u>000</u>

EXAMPLES

▶ 4100 ÷ 10 = 410
500 ÷ 100 = 5

Exercise 8A

1	3 × 100	**2**	7 × 1000	**3**	11 × 100	**4**	120 ÷ 10
5	3700 ÷ 100	**6**	2000 ÷ 10	**7**	32 × 10	**8**	71 × 1000
9	4500 ÷ 100	**10**	3010 ÷ 10	**11**	68 × 10	**12**	6 × 1000
13	29 × 100	**14**	8000 ÷ 100	**15**	75 000 ÷ 1000	**16**	2780 ÷ 10
17	172 × 100	**18**	910 × 10	**19**	5 × 1000	**20**	83 000 ÷ 100
21	52 000 ÷ 1000	**22**	27 000 ÷ 10	**23**	85 × 100	**24**	4 × 1000
25	700 000 ÷ 100	**26**	1500 ÷ 10	**27**	45 × 100	**28**	130 × 100
29	9700 ÷ 100	**30**	11 000 ÷ 1000				

Exercise 8B

1	9 × 10	**2**	17 × 1000	**3**	65 × 100	**4**	3000 ÷ 1000
5	4000 ÷ 100	**6**	78 000 ÷ 10	**7**	84 × 100	**8**	16 × 1000

9 403×10	**10** $5600 \div 100$	**11** $63\,000 \div 1000$	**12** $48\,200 \div 10$
13 18×1000	**14** 632×100	**15** 44×10	**16** $9700 \div 10$
17 $18\,000 \div 100$	**18** $31\,000 \div 1000$	**19** 260×10	**20** 306×100
21 800×1000	**22** $5\,000\,000 \div 1000$	**23** $1900 \div 10$	**24** $50\,600 \div 100$
25 20×100	**26** 5700×100	**27** $60\,000 \div 100$	**28** $51\,000 \div 1000$
29 733×100	**30** $75\,000 \times 1000$		

9/ MULTIPLICATION BY A 2-DIGIT NUMBER WITHOUT A CALCULATOR

When multiplying by a number such as 27, it is important to remember that the '2' is 2 tens (or twenty).

When multiplying by 20, remember to put a nought at the end and multiply by 2.

EXAMPLE

▶ $132 \times 27 = 3564$

$$
\begin{array}{r}
1\ 3\ 2 \\
\times\quad 2\ 7 \\
\hline
9\ 2\ 4 \\
2\ 6\ 4\ 0 \\
\hline
3\ 5\ 6\ 4 \\
\end{array}
$$

Exercise 9A

1 106×11	**2** 142×13	**3** 231×12	**4** 314×15	**5** 112×14
6 353×12	**7** 109×13	**8** 175×16	**9** 404×14	**10** 136×13
11 512×16	**12** 157×23	**13** 427×21	**14** 357×22	**15** 640×17
16 743×19	**17** 383×18	**18** 824×23	**19** 658×24	**20** 846×61
21 745×25	**22** 374×19	**23** 572×31	**24** 477×71	**25** 927×55
26 896×83	**27** 746×41	**28** 638×52	**29** 919×91	**30** 833×35

Exercise 9B

1 125×13	**2** 116×11	**3** 145×12	**4** 221×14	**5** 153×13
6 315×15	**7** 132×16	**8** 213×14	**9** 506×16	**10** 463×15
11 421×22	**12** 204×21	**13** 162×23	**14** 416×25	**15** 309×27
16 182×31	**17** 643×32	**18** 708×41	**19** 791×62	**20** 925×21
21 362×25	**22** 940×34	**23** 675×37	**24** 561×81	**25** 298×43
26 908×51	**27** 682×44	**28** 724×92	**29** 609×71	**30** 729×63

10/ DIVISION BY A 2-DIGIT NUMBER WITHOUT A CALCULATOR

When dividing by a number that is bigger than 10, long division can be used. This is better for this type of division than short division but is not essential as both methods will give the correct answer. If you prefer, use short division but, if you are able to use long division, keep practising; it is worth the effort.

EXAMPLE

▶ $777 \div 21 = 37$

$$
\begin{array}{r}
3\ 7 \\
21\overline{)7\ 7\ 7} \\
-\ 6\ 3 \\
\hline
1\ 4\ 7 \\
-\ 1\ 4\ 7 \\
\hline
0
\end{array}
$$

Exercise 10A

1 $143 \div 11$	**2** $195 \div 15$	**3** $108 \div 12$	**4** $165 \div 11$	**5** $195 \div 13$
6 $132 \div 11$	**7** $198 \div 18$	**8** $132 \div 22$	**9** $121 \div 11$	**10** $192 \div 16$
11 $221 \div 13$	**12** $156 \div 12$	**13** $133 \div 19$	**14** $225 \div 25$	**15** $348 \div 29$
16 $270 \div 45$	**17** $384 \div 32$	**18** $338 \div 26$	**19** $315 \div 21$	**20** $528 \div 16$
21 $377 \div 13$	**22** $819 \div 63$	**23** $444 \div 74$	**24** $319 \div 29$	**25** $434 \div 31$
26 $510 \div 85$	**27** $236 \div 59$	**28** $196 \div 49$	**29** $693 \div 99$	**30** $495 \div 33$

Exercise 10B

1 $154 \div 11$	**2** $312 \div 13$	**3** $180 \div 12$	**4** $240 \div 15$	**5** $187 \div 17$
6 $208 \div 16$	**7** $253 \div 23$	**8** $385 \div 11$	**9** $189 \div 21$	**10** $286 \div 22$
11 $341 \div 31$	**12** $288 \div 24$	**13** $242 \div 22$	**14** $217 \div 31$	**15** $396 \div 33$
16 $352 \div 32$	**17** $375 \div 25$	**18** $209 \div 19$	**19** $377 \div 29$	**20** $273 \div 21$
21 $324 \div 18$	**22** $323 \div 17$	**23** $465 \div 15$	**24** $2016 \div 72$	**25** $1200 \div 48$
26 $306 \div 51$	**27** $552 \div 69$	**28** $345 \div 23$	**29** $1748 \div 92$	**30** $979 \div 89$

11/ SIMPLE FACTORS

What two numbers can be multiplied together to give an answer of 24?

There are several choices. There are 2×12, 3×8 and 4×6 but 12×2, 8×3 and 6×4 also work. There is also 1×24 or 24×1 but do not use these in this exercise.

EXAMPLE

▶ Write two examples of a pair of factors that can be multiplied together to give 30. Do not use 1×30 as an example. Choose *different* numbers for your second example.

$3 \times 10 = 30$ and $5 \times 6 = 30$ (Note: You could have used 2×15.)

Exercise 11A

Write down *one* example of a pair of factors which can be multiplied together to give each of the stated numbers. Do *not* use 1 as a factor.

1 16	**2** 30	**3** 44	**4** 60	**5** 20	**6** 78
7 65	**8** 46	**9** 15	**10** 36	**11** 50	**12** 84

13 57	**14** 28	**15** 86	**16** 125	**17** 108	**18** 93
19 72	**20** 62	**21** 120	**22** 90	**23** 63	**24** 105
25 144	**26** 114	**27** 66	**28** 136	**29** 69	**30** 250

Exercise 11B

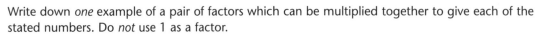

Write down *one* example of a pair of factors which can be multiplied together to give each of the stated numbers. Do *not* use 1 as a factor.

1 18	**2** 8	**3** 42	**4** 58	**5** 12	**6** 32
7 52	**8** 24	**9** 80	**10** 68	**11** 48	**12** 100
13 40	**14** 51	**15** 64	**16** 82	**17** 56	**18** 81
19 54	**20** 87	**21** 150	**22** 110	**23** 95	**24** 70
25 112	**26** 106	**27** 124	**28** 160	**29** 115	**30** 132

Exercises 11C and 11D

(These can be used as an alternative to or as revision of Exercises 11A and 11B.)

Write down *two* examples (where possible) of a pair of factors which can be multiplied together to give the stated number in each question of Exercises 11A and B or, if you have just completed Exercise 11A or B, give one more example of a pair of factors for each question (where possible).

Do not make your second example the reverse of the first, for example *not* 5 × 6 with 6 × 5.

Do *not* use 1 as a factor.

12/ THE VALUE OF A GIVEN DIGIT WITHIN A NUMBER

The value of a digit in a number depends upon its position within that number.

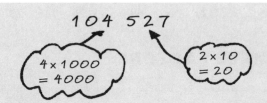

EXAMPLE

▶ State the value of the underlined digits in number form: 3̲2̲5 641

The 3 has the value 300 000.   The 2 has the value 20 000.

EXAMPLE

▶ State the value of the underlined digits in word form: 5̲ 100 2̲41

The 5 has the value five million.   The 2 has the value two hundred.

Exercise 12A

Write the value of the underlined digits in **number form.**

1 25̲ 162	**2** 815 3̲42	**3** 6̲52 401	**4** 63 4̲55	**5** 298 4̲10
6 5 8̲97	**7** 5̲12 896	**8** 2̲ 560 050	**9** 3̲ 565 258	**10** 205 6̲84
11 17̲ 643	**12** 5̲ 000 56̲2	**13** 1̲2 300 650	**14** 825 6̲34	**15** 3 45̲0 633

Write the value of the underlined digits in **word form**.

16	21 <u>6</u>50	**17**	43 9<u>8</u>8	**18**	195 <u>4</u>30	**19**	205 <u>6</u>07	**20**	989 <u>2</u>35
21	1 <u>05</u>0 500	**22**	13 2<u>3</u>4	**23**	5<u>64</u> 335	**24**	<u>2</u>1 000 000	**25**	452 <u>6</u>78
26	98 <u>7</u>76	**27**	<u>3</u> 117 489	**28**	<u>17</u> 452 322	**29**	411 1<u>2</u>1	**30**	7 <u>500</u> 300

Exercise 12B

Write the value of the underlined digits in **number form.**

1	19 <u>7</u>65	**2**	25 1<u>4</u>7	**3**	2<u>2</u>5 338	**4**	<u>7</u>02 185	**5**	13 <u>5</u>60
6	<u>4</u> 604 576	**7**	1<u>45</u> 261	**8**	78 <u>5</u>64	**9**	11 <u>4</u>45 200	**10**	625 <u>8</u>72
11	27 <u>4</u>13	**12**	<u>5</u> 632 500	**13**	20<u>5</u> 745 500	**14**	1<u>1</u>2 458	**15**	2 6<u>50</u> 157

Write the value of the underlined digits in **word form**.

16	13 <u>5</u>41	**17**	156 <u>4</u>47	**18**	<u>5</u>26 894	**19**	<u>7</u>1 598	**20**	8 <u>5</u>56
21	2<u>2</u>6 841	**22**	8 <u>9</u>00 000	**23**	568 <u>1</u>17	**24**	<u>6</u>5 752	**25**	453 <u>6</u>21
26	4<u>5</u> 000 000	**27**	1<u>78</u> 566	**28**	6 <u>5</u>07 000	**29**	56 <u>3</u>45	**30**	5 <u>452</u> 000

13/ ESTIMATING THE ANSWERS TO ADDITIONS AND SUBTRACTIONS

EXAMPLE

▶ Estimate the answer to 503 + 198 and then add the two numbers to see if the estimation was good.

As 503 is approximately 500 and 198 is
approximately 200, this means that the answer
is approximately 500 + 200 = 700.

$$\begin{array}{r} 503 \\ +198 \\ \hline 701 \end{array}$$

The exact answer is 701 which means that the approximation was very good.

EXAMPLE

▶ By approximating to the nearest 10, estimate the answer to 82 + 71.

This is approximately
80 + 70 = 150.

EXAMPLE

▶ By approximating to the nearest 100, estimate the answer to 434 − 158.

This is approximately
400 − 200 = 200.

Exercise 13A

In each of the following questions, (a) estimate the answer by approximating the numbers to the nearest 10, (b) complete the calculation and compare the answer with your estimate.

1	213 + 174	**2**	187 + 114	**3**	173 − 118	**4**	94 − 27	**5**	433 + 128
6	171 + 83	**7**	322 − 297	**8**	165 − 82	**9**	114 + 86	**10**	298 − 195

In each of the following questions, (a) estimate the answer by approximating the numbers to the nearest 100, (b) complete the calculation and compare the answer with your estimate.

11 356 + 191 **12** 477 + 394 **13** 876 − 245 **14** 1010 + 415
15 1209 − 942 **16** 377 + 761 **17** 1285 − 465 **18** 1830 − 727
19 818 + 326 **20** 1570 − 1245

Exercise 13B

In each of the following questions, (a) estimate the answer by approximating the numbers to the nearest 10, (b) complete the calculation and compare the answer with your estimate.

1 92 + 73 **2** 157 − 88 **3** 520 − 99 **4** 114 + 216 **5** 611 − 497
6 236 + 109 **7** 333 + 86 **8** 182 + 94 **9** 233 − 124 **10** 458 + 229

In each of the following questions, (a) estimate the answer by approximating the numbers to the nearest 100, (b) complete the calculation and compare the answer with your estimate.

11 366 + 289 **12** 1109 − 884 **13** 1259 − 915 **14** 987 + 179
15 1550 − 767 **16** 2332 − 1995 **17** 1367 + 885 **18** 1422 − 675
19 1108 + 694 **20** 1089 − 982

14/ DIVISION AND MULTIPLICATION AS INVERSE OPERATIONS WITH AND WITHOUT A CALCULATOR

$6 \times 7 = 42$ and $42 \div 7 = 6$

If 6 is multiplied by 7, the answer is 42. If this answer (42) is divided by 7, the answer is 6 again. Multiplication and division are inverse operations, that is, they are opposites.

Exercise 14A

Pair each of the multiplications 1, 2, 3 etc. with one of the divisions A, B, C etc., for example, 1 is paired with J.

1 8 × 3 **2** 3 × 9 **3** 8 × 4 **4** 6 × 7 **5** 11 × 5
6 15 × 4 **7** 4 × 6 **8** 9 × 6 **9** 6 × 5 **10** 10 × 2
11 12 × 5 **12** 9 × 3 **13** 8 × 8 **14** 8 × 7 **15** 6 × 8
16 13 × 3 **17** 12 × 4 **18** 5 × 9 **19** 15 × 3 **20** 16 × 5

A 42 ÷ 7 **B** 56 ÷ 7 **C** 55 ÷ 5 **D** 32 ÷ 4 **E** 64 ÷ 8
F 54 ÷ 6 **G** 60 ÷ 4 **H** 60 ÷ 5 **I** 45 ÷ 9 **J** 24 ÷ 3
K 45 ÷ 3 **L** 39 ÷ 3 **M** 27 ÷ 9 **N** 24 ÷ 6 **O** 30 ÷ 5
P 20 ÷ 2 **Q** 48 ÷ 4 **R** 48 ÷ 8 **S** 80 ÷ 5 **T** 27 ÷ 3

Exercise 14B

Pair each of the multiplications 1, 2, 3 etc. with one of the divisions A, B, C etc., for example,
1 is paired with K.

1 7×3	**2** 7×4	**3** 9×5	**4** 5×6	**5** 5×8
6 7×5	**7** 4×6	**8** 9×4	**9** 7×8	**10** 7×6
11 13×4	**12** 12×8	**13** 17×3	**14** 11×9	**15** 11×4
16 13×5	**17** 13×9	**18** 16×3	**19** 17×7	**20** 19×5

A $40 \div 8$	**B** $65 \div 5$	**C** $45 \div 5$	**D** $52 \div 4$	**E** $30 \div 6$
F $48 \div 3$	**G** $24 \div 6$	**H** $96 \div 8$	**I** $44 \div 4$	**J** $51 \div 3$
K $21 \div 3$	**L** $42 \div 6$	**M** $117 \div 9$	**N** $35 \div 5$	**O** $99 \div 9$
P $28 \div 4$	**Q** $95 \div 5$	**R** $56 \div 8$	**S** $36 \div 4$	**T** $119 \div 7$

Exercise 14C

Pair each of the multiplications 1, 2, 3 etc. with one of the divisions A, B, C etc.

1 175×21	**2** 332×32	**3** 192×13	**4** 249×15
5 175×23	**6** 311×17	**7** 187×13	**8** 192×32
9 177×21	**10** 321×35	**11** 261×15	**12** 195×23
13 311×25	**14** 332×35	**15** 249×25	**16** 187×32
17 261×17	**18** 177×22	**19** 321×17	**20** 195×22

A $2431 \div 13$	**B** $3735 \div 15$	**C** $3915 \div 15$	**D** $5457 \div 1$
E $3675 \div 21$	**F** $7775 \div 25$	**G** $4290 \div 22$	**H** $3717 \div 21$
I $6225 \div 25$	**J** $4437 \div 17$	**K** $11\,235 \div 35$	**L** $5287 \div 17$
M $10\,624 \div 32$	**N** $4025 \div 23$	**O** $11\,620 \div 35$	**P** $2496 \div 13$
Q $6144 \div 32$	**R** $3894 \div 22$	**S** $5984 \div 32$	**T** $4485 \div 23$

Exercise 14D

Pair each of the multiplications 1, 2, 3 etc. with one of the divisions A, B, C etc.

1 619×21	**2** 359×13	**3** 564×21	**4** 357×17
5 413×15	**6** 615×18	**7** 349×13	**8** 626×21
9 615×23	**10** 409×25	**11** 409×15	**12** 564×17
13 619×18	**14** 359×21	**15** 357×15	**16** 349×23
17 413×25	**18** 626×18	**19** 575×23	**20** 575×17

A $11\,070 \div 18$	**B** $12\,999 \div 21$	**C** $9775 \div 17$	**D** $9588 \div 17$
E $11\,268 \div 18$	**F** $11\,844 \div 21$	**G** $13\,146 \div 21$	**H** $5355 \div 15$
I $13\,225 \div 23$	**J** $10\,225 \div 25$	**K** $7539 \div 21$	**L** $6195 \div 15$
M $4667 \div 13$	**N** $10\,325 \div 25$	**O** $11\,142 \div 18$	**P** $14\,145 \div 23$
Q $8027 \div 23$	**R** $6069 \div 17$	**S** $4537 \div 13$	**T** $6135 \div 15$

15/ DIVISION TO THE NEAREST WHOLE NUMBER WITH AND WITHOUT A CALCULATOR

These exercises are about dividing and then knowing whether to **round up** or **round down** to the nearest whole number.

$48 \div 6 = 8$ exactly.

$50 \div 6 = 8$ remainder 2 (using mental arithmetic) or 8.3333333333 (using a calculator).

If the answer is required to the nearest whole number, round *down* to 8.

This is because the remainder 2 is less than half of 6 and 8.333333333333 is less than 8.5 (which is halfway between 8 and 9).

$51 \div 6 = 8$ remainder 3 (mental arithmetic) or 8.5 (calculator).

When the answer is exactly halfway between two numbers, the rule is to round *up*.

Thus $51 \div 6$ has an answer of 9 (to the nearest whole number).

Without a calculator

> **EXAMPLE**
>
> ▶ $95 \div 9 = 10$ remainder 5
>   = 11 (to the nearest whole number)
> The remainder of 5 is more than half of the number 9 by which you are dividing, so round *up* to 11.

With a calculator

> **EXAMPLE**
>
> ▶ $66 \div 7 = 9.4285714$
>   = 9 (to the nearest whole number)
> 9.5 is halfway between 9 and 10.
> 9.4285714 is less than 9.5 so round *down* to 9.

Exercise 15A

Calculate these divisions to the nearest whole number.

1 $19 \div 3$	**2** $24 \div 5$	**3** $27 \div 4$	**4** $32 \div 6$	**5** $25 \div 3$
6 $21 \div 2$	**7** $26 \div 5$	**8** $44 \div 6$	**9** $31 \div 4$	**10** $20 \div 3$
11 $34 \div 4$	**12** $81 \div 5$	**13** $45 \div 4$	**14** $51 \div 5$	**15** $26 \div 6$
16 $37 \div 6$	**17** $17 \div 6$	**18** $52 \div 3$	**19** $57 \div 6$	**20** $19 \div 5$

Exercise 15B

Calculate these divisions to the nearest whole number.

1 $34 \div 5$	**2** $25 \div 2$	**3** $38 \div 3$	**4** $43 \div 4$	**5** $76 \div 7$
6 $23 \div 8$	**7** $16 \div 3$	**8** $31 \div 5$	**9** $29 \div 4$	**10** $37 \div 3$
11 $20 \div 6$	**12** $42 \div 4$	**13** $23 \div 6$	**14** $32 \div 3$	**15** $38 \div 6$
16 $49 \div 4$	**17** $30 \div 4$	**18** $44 \div 3$	**19** $75 \div 6$	**20** $48 \div 5$

Exercise 15C

Work out these divisions to the nearest whole number (using a calculator).

1	145 ÷ 7	**2**	200 ÷ 9	**3**	135 ÷ 8	**4**	298 ÷ 11	**5**	157 ÷ 12
6	307 ÷ 15	**7**	288 ÷ 17	**8**	500 ÷ 14	**9**	410 ÷ 16	**10**	1002 ÷ 21
11	1133 ÷ 18	**12**	2050 ÷ 17	**13**	508 ÷ 19	**14**	199 ÷ 13	**15**	1209 ÷ 16
16	577 ÷ 24	**17**	413 ÷ 14	**18**	644 ÷ 11	**19**	795 ÷ 27	**20**	1136 ÷ 19

Exercise 15D

Work out these divisions to the nearest whole number (using a calculator).

1	214 ÷ 9	**2**	199 ÷ 12	**3**	250 ÷ 13	**4**	758 ÷ 15	**5**	319 ÷ 14
6	599 ÷ 17	**7**	2015 ÷ 21	**8**	634 ÷ 23	**9**	178 ÷ 19	**10**	280 ÷ 22
11	381 ÷ 18	**12**	2930 ÷ 17	**13**	380 ÷ 13	**14**	448 ÷ 24	**15**	999 ÷ 18
16	17826 ÷ 23	**17**	2642 ÷ 28	**18**	3125 ÷ 15	**19**	807 ÷ 18	**20**	4215 ÷ 26

16/ PROBLEMS INVOLVING ADDITION, SUBTRACTION, MULTIPLICATION AND DIVISION WITHOUT A CALCULATOR

In these two exercises you must not use a calculator. If you need to do any calculations, show these neatly and clearly with your work.

EXAMPLE

► In a sale the price of a new coat is reduced by £7.54. If the original price was £50.27, what is the price in the sale?

New price = £50.27 − £7.54
= £42.73

$$\begin{array}{r} £50.27 \\ -£7.54 \\ \hline £\,42.73 \end{array}$$

Exercise 16A

1 Terry needs 75 cm of tape at the top of each curtain. How much does she need for four curtains?

2 I cut a 76-cm length of timber into four equal pieces. What is the length of each piece?

3 Ashok takes 7 minutes walking to the bus stop. He waits 5 minutes for a bus which takes 12 minutes to reach town. What is the total time taken?

4 Seven sweets weigh a total of 84 grams. What is the weight of each sweet?

5 Jack has £10. He spends £6.25. How much does he have left?

6 The price of a pair of scissors is £9.99 plus £2.50 post and packing. What is the total cost?

7 If 60 students need to be split up into four equal groups, how many should there be in each group?

8 Subtract 17 from 65 and then multiply by 6.

9 Divide 75 by 5 and then multiply your answer by 7.

10 There are eight tiles in a box. How many boxes will be needed if you require 50 tiles?

11 The price of a TV is reduced from £205 to £149. How much is the reduction?

12 How much change should you receive from £20 if you spend £7.26?

13 What is the total cost of nine packs of beefburgers at £1.72 each?

14 A bottle contains 440 ml of washing-up liquid. How much do three bottles hold?

15 Pens are packed with six pens in each box. How many boxes can be filled from a case of 80 pens?

16 The total of two angles is 180°. If one of the angles is 45°, what is the other angle?

17 Add 67 and 32 and multiply the answer by 8.

18 Divide 76 by 4 and then multiply by 5.

19 Subtract 46 from 100 and then multiply the answer by 6.

20 Multiply 34 by 9 and then add 56.

Exercise 16B

1 Molly receives £4 profit on every soft toy that she makes. How many toys does she have to make in order to gain £92 profit?

2 A panel of fencing requires thirteen metres of timber. What length of timber is required for seven panels?

3 Picture pins are packed in packs of four. How many packs are needed if 30 pins are required?

4 How many minutes are there in four hours?

5 If there are five pens in a pack, how many pens are there in 14 packs?

6 Rachel trips whilst carrying 24 eggs. Seven remain unbroken. How many eggs did Rachel break?

7 All the cartons in the diagram have the same width. What is the width of each carton?

8 Beth sells her bicycle for £25 and a computer game for £6 but has to give her brother £11. How much money does she have left?

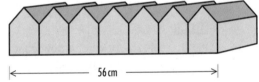

56 cm

9 Party glasses are packed in boxes of six. How many glasses are there in 36 boxes?

10 Tony has £11.50. He earns £7.50 but spends £9.50. How much does he have left?

11 Dog food is packed in boxes each of which contains 24 cans. How many cans are there in nine boxes?

12 Sheets of card are packed with five in a pack. How many packs can be made from 144 sheets?

13 If 142 people buy tickets for a performance and 98 pay at the door, how many people watch the performance?

14 Seven boxes contain 343 matches. How many are in each box if each contains the same number?

15 Gillian has read 78 pages of a book containing 205 pages. How many pages does Gillian have left to read?

16 Glasses are packed in boxes of six. How many boxes are needed for 330 glasses?

17 If there are 36 packs of paper in a box, how many packs are there in four boxes?

18 Jenny scores 89, 86 and 95 in three tests. What is her total score?

19 Subtract 48 from 97 and then multiply by 7.

20 Add 126 and 195 and then divide by 3.

17/ PROBLEMS INVOLVING ADDITION, SUBTRACTION, MULTIPLICATION AND DIVISION WITH A CALCULATOR

In these two exercises you are expected to use a calculator. It is essential to read the question and decide which of the following you need: $+$, $-$, $\div$ or $\times$. Make up your mind and be sure to *write down* the calculation that you intend to perform using your calculator.

EXAMPLE

▶ How many plastic forks are there in 13 boxes each containing 144 forks?

Number of forks $= 144 \times 13$
$= 1872$ forks

Exercise 17A

1. There are 22 biscuits in a packet. How many biscuits are there in 15 packets?

2. Claire works for 6 hours 30 minutes. How many minutes is this?

3. Disks are packed in boxes of 12. How many boxes can be filled from a case of 200 disks?

4. A can of paint covers 15 square metres of wall. How many square metres will 11 cans cover?

5. An aeroplane has seats for 132 passengers. There are 47 empty seats. How many passengers are there?

6. Navid lists his earnings for four weeks. He earns £132.65, £118.75, £109.38 and £137.80. How much did he earn altogether?

7. There are eighteen dish-cloths in each pack. How many packs are required in order to have at least 200 dish-cloths?

8. Susan has £345.01 in her bank account. How much will she have left if she pays a telephone bill for £136.22?

9. How many 15-ml doses of medicine are there in a 360-ml bottle?

10. What is the total cost of 12 cans of spaghetti at 28p per can?

11. Each office in an office block has windows containing 24 panes of glass. How many panes of glass are there in the windows of 21 offices?

12. Dean drives 139 km before he has a break. He then drives a further 94 km. How far does he drive altogether?

13. Jenny earns £117.48 but has to pay out £42.64. How much does she have left?

14. There are 16 tiles in a box. How many boxes do you need if you require 100 tiles?

15. The Khan family have seven rolls of film; each of these can be used to take 24 photographs. They also have three rolls of film for 36 photographs. How many photographs can they take between them?

16. There are 16 peaches in each pack in a shop. How many packs are required in order to have at least 120 peaches?

17. There are 14 buttons on each of 24 cards of buttons. How many buttons are there in total?

18. Kentaro earns £326 for doing some work but has to pay £165.69 for materials. How much of the money remains?

19 How many days are there in five years if two of the years are leap years?

20 There are eighteen pencils in each box. How many boxes are required in order to have at least 150 pencils?

Exercise 17B

1 Helen earns £187.63 but has to pay tax of £44.78. How much remains?

2 Julie earns £3.50 per hour. How many hours will she need to work in order to earn £42?

3 Brushes are sold in packs of three. Each pack costs £4.49. What will be the total cost of 48 brushes?

4 Gary has £98.65 in savings but takes out £45.27 to pay for a personal stereo. How much money does he have left?

5 There are 12 755 people in one stand at a match and 11 736 in another stand. What is the total for the two stands?

6 Cat food is sold in cases of 12. How many cases do you need to buy in order to have at least 80 tins?

7 The cost of my train ticket is £37.67 and the cost of my taxi to the station is £5.28. What is the total cost?

8 How much medicine is left in a bottle which contained 360 ml if 125 ml has been used?

9 The safety limit on a lift is 1000 kg. Is it safe for fourteen people each weighing 75 kg to travel in the lift?

10 Tim is paid £147.45 for a week's work. He gets a bonus payment of £45.63. How much does he earn in total?

11 Jack owes £442. How many weeks does it take him to pay the money back at £17 per week?

12 Gavin knows that he needs to drive 285 km. How much further is remaining after he has driven 98 km?

13 There are 300 tins in the store. Adam puts 144 of these on the shelves. How many tins remain?

14 Georgina earns £75.24 and £18.95. How much is this in total?

15 Decorations are packed in boxes of 15. How many boxes can be filled from a case of 200 decorations?

16 Some curtains need 95 cm of material each. What length of material is required for 14 curtains?

17 Emma notes the number of hours that she works in each of three months. She works 117, 89 and 124 hours. How many hours is this in total?

18 A shopkeeper buys rolls of tape in packs of twelve. A box contains 2880 rolls. How many packs are in each box?

19 There are 24 traffic cones on every 120 metres of motorway. How many cones are needed for 600 metres?

20 Emma completes a race in thirteen minutes less than 3 hours. How many minutes is this?

REVISION

Exercise A

Questions 1–8 are for mental arithmetic. Write the answers only (without any working out).

1 (a) 35 + 26   (b) 75 − 37   (c) 51 − 12   (d) 27 + 26

2 (a) 7 + 4 − 6 + 3   (b) 8 − 2 − 7 + 2   (c) 9 + 6 − 8 + 4   (d) 2 − 7 + 6 + 5

3 Write the following in words:
(a) 9354   (b) 23 985   (c) 617 150   (d) 3 500 455

4 Write the following in number form:
(a) Four thousand, five hundred and thirty-six
(b) Nineteen thousand, three hundred and seventy-seven
(c) One hundred and three thousand, five hundred and sixty-seven
(d) Five million, four hundred thousand

5 (a) 5×7 (b) 4×6 (c) 8×9 (d) 7×6
    (e) 4×9 (f) 5×8 (g) 6×9 (h) 9×7

6 (a) 76×1000 (b) 179×100 (c) $9000 \div 100$ (d) $88\,000 \div 1000$

7 Write down *two* examples of a pair of factors which, when multiplied together, give each of the stated numbers. Do *not* use 1 as a factor.
(a) 36   (b) 20

8 Write the value of the underlined digits in *number* form.
(a) 35 2<u>6</u>2   (b) 816 <u>5</u>33   (c) <u>7</u>22 607   (d) <u>7</u>9 4<u>3</u>5

The following questions should be answered without the use of a calculator but you should show any working that you find necessary.

9 (a) 45×7 (b) $57 \div 3$ (c) $95 \div 5$ (d) 38×6

10 (a) 407×15 (b) 314×21 (c) $564 \div 12$ (d) $391 \div 23$

11 Estimate the answer to each question by approximating the numbers to the nearest 10.
(a) $132 + 47$ (b) $119 - 63$

12 Work out these divisions to the nearest whole number.
(a) $22 \div 3$ (b) $32 \div 5$ (c) $54 \div 7$ (d) $35 \div 4$

Exercise AA

1 A newspaper reports that the number of people at two weekend ice-hockey games was one thousand, four hundred and sixty-five on Saturday and one thousand, nine hundred and seventy-four on Sunday.
What is the total for the two games in words?

2 A company employs two thousand, five hundred and twelve people. If seven hundred and eighteen of these are on holiday or ill, how many remain? (You may answer in number form.)

3 What is the total weight of 24 parcels each weighing 348 grams?

4 How many 18-cm lengths can be cut from a 3-metre length of material?

5 Frank thinks of two numbers which, when multiplied together, give an answer of 72. State three examples of such pairs of numbers?

6 Nicole earns £213.56 before deductions. She has deductions of £57.15. How much does she have remaining after these deductions have been taken from her earnings?

7 Daniel has seven weeks to save £61. How much does he need to save each week to the nearest pound?

8 The takings at a small shop over a five-day period are £145.68, £109.87, £99.56, £175.31 and £122.61. What is the total?

9 A car driver calculates that she can travel 13.5 miles for every litre of petrol. How many miles can she travel on 38 litres?

10 It takes 17 minutes for Neville to paint a vase. How many vases can he paint in 5 hours 40 minutes?

18/ NUMBER LINES

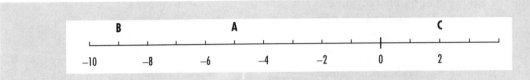

EXAMPLE
► State the reading at the positions marked A and B.

A is at −5 and B at −9.

EXAMPLE
► How far is it from A to C?

It is 7 units from A to C.

Exercise 18A

State the value at each of the points marked with a letter.

1

2

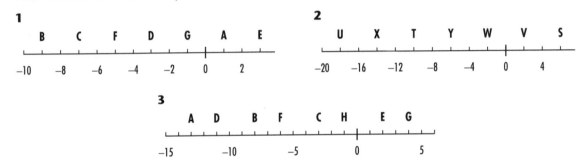

3

4

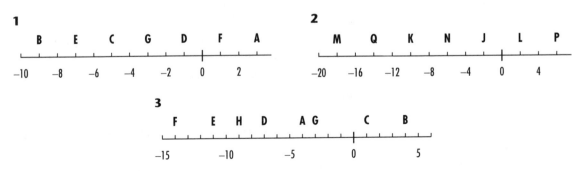

State how far it is between the following points:

(a) A to D   (b) F to L   (c) M to Q
(d) S to V   (e) E to K   (f) J to U
(g) F to R   (h) P to U   (i) B to L
(j) A to F   (k) G to M   (l) C to J

Exercise 18B

State the value at each of the points marked with a letter.

1

2

3

4

State how far it is between the following points:

(a) D to J   (b) L to R   (c) F to L

(d) A to G   (e) G to J   (f) K to N

(g) Q to R   (h) H to T   (i) A to E

(j) E to R   (k) J to M   (l) C to L

Exercise 18C

State the value at each of the points marked with a letter.

1

2

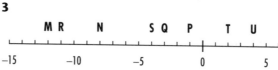

3

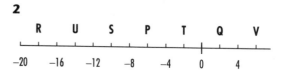

4

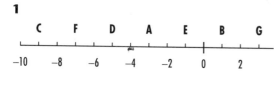

State how far it is between the pairs of values given.

(a) −9 and −7   (b) −10 and −5

(c) −5 and − 4   (d) −1 and +1

(e) −4 and +4   (f) −6 and 0

(g) +3 and +7   (h) −10 and +1

Exercise 18D

State the value at each of the points marked with a letter.

1

2

3

4

State how far it is between the pairs of values given.

(a) −4 and −1   (b) −5 and −1

(c) −9 and −3   (d) −3 and +2

(e) −1 and +3   (f) −7 and −1

(g) −2 and +4   (h) −8 and +2

19/ ORDERING NUMBERS THAT INCLUDE NEGATIVE NUMBERS

EXAMPLE

▶ Rewrite the following numbers in ascending order of size: 3, –2, –5, 0, 1, –3

The number –5 is the smallest and 3 is the largest (3 means +3).
So, in order of size: –5, –3, –2, 0, 1, 3

Remember: Ascending order means 'smallest first with numbers increasing in size'.
Descending order means 'largest first with numbers getting smaller'.

Exercise 19A

Rewrite the numbers in the order stated.

1	–1, 2, –2, 1	ascending		**2**	4, 1, 0, –3	ascending
3	3, –1, –2, 1	descending		**4**	–1, 0, –2, 2	descending
5	–3, –2, –1, –4	ascending		**6**	6, 3, –1, 0	ascending
7	0, –1, 1, –2	descending		**8**	5, 0, 2, –1	descending
9	–4, –5, –3, –2	ascending		**10**	–1, –3, –5, 0	ascending
11	–5, –2, –3, –1	descending		**12**	–1, 1, –2, 2	descending
13	3, –11, 0, –8, –2	ascending		**14**	5, 7, –2, –4, –3	descending
15	–1, 0, 1, –2, 3	descending		**16**	0, –2, 3, –3, –1	ascending
17	1, –2, –1, 4, –3	descending		**18**	–5, –3, –1, 0, –4	ascending
19	2, –1, 5, 1, –3	descending		**20**	3, 0, –2, –1, –5	ascending
21	–1, 2, –3, –2, 0, 1	descending		**22**	12, 9, –9, 8, –7, 0	ascending
23	23, 24, 11, –1, –2, 0	descending		**24**	–1, 12, 11, –11, –12, 7	descending
25	–19, –21, –3, 3, 0, 5	ascending		**26**	–225, –195, –10, –11, –13, –99 descending
27	335, 625, –124, –87, –56, 346 descending		**28**	–2, –5, –4, –6, –8, 0, 1	ascending
29	0, 3, 1, –2, –1, –3, –5	ascending		**30**	3, –2, –3, 2, 1, 0, –1	descending

Exercise 19B

Rewrite the numbers in the order stated.

1	–1, 0, –2, 2	descending		**2**	4, 0, 5, –1	descending
3	–2, 0, –3, 2	ascending		**4**	–1, –2, –3, –4	ascending
5	3, –3, –1, 1	descending		**6**	2, 3, –2, –1	descending
7	–3, 0, –2, 5	ascending		**8**	–1, 0, –5, 1	ascending
9	2, –4, 6, –1	descending		**10**	–2, 0, –3, 1	descending
11	2, –4, –3, –5	ascending		**12**	0, 1, –1, –3	ascending
13	–5, –4, 2, –1, 0	descending		**14**	2, –1, –6, 4, 3	ascending
15	10, –2, 9, –7, –6	ascending		**16**	4, –3, –1, 0, 2	descending

17	–5, –3, –1, 0, –2 descending	**18**	7, 0, 6, –1, 2 ascending
19	–1, 1, 0, 5, –2 descending	**20**	–2, –1, –3, –4, 0 descending
21	13, 7, –1, 8, –4, –2 ascending	**22**	–7, –5, 0, 1, –1, –2 ascending
23	6, –5, 4, –3, 2, –1 descending	**24**	0, –2, 2, –3, 3, –1 ascending
25	–12, –10, –13, –9, –8, –14 ascending	**26**	–15, –20, 10, –25, 5, –5 descending
27	–137, –136, –140, –127, –99, –95 descending	**28**	1, –3, 0, –5, 4, –2, –1 ascending
29	–5, –7, 1, 0, –6, –2, –4 ascending	**30**	2, –1, –2, 1, –3, 3, 0 descending

20/ NEGATIVE NUMBERS IN CONTEXT

EXAMPLE

▶ A man was born in 12 BCE and died after his birthday in 45 CE. How old was he when he died?

Note: BCE is another way of saying BC, and CE can be used for AD.

The year 12 BCE can be thought of as (–12) and the year 45 CE as (+45).
So, (–12) to (+45) = 12 + 45 = 57
He was 57 years old.

EXAMPLE

▶ Suhana arrived 14 minutes before her bus should have left but the bus was half an hour late. How long did she have to wait?

The 14 minutes is added to the 30 minutes since the times are either side of the correct arrival time.
She had to wait 44 minutes.

Exercise 20A

1 The temperature was 7°C before it dropped by 9°C. What is the new temperature?

2 What year is 15 years before 5 BCE?

3 The temperature changed from –2°C to –5°C. Did the temperature rise or fall and by how much did it change?

4 Kerry owes the bank £124. She pays in £78. How much does she owe now?

5 My watch shows 5 minutes to 12 but my watch is 11 minutes slow. What is the real time?

6 The temperature was –2°C before it rose by 3°C. What is the new temperature?

7 A woman born in 11 BCE died after her birthday in 25 CE. How old was she when she died?

8 Ash Fen is 17 metres below sea-level. Ash Rise is 3 metres above sea-level. What is the difference in level between Ash Rise and Ash Fen?

9 Stephen owes £56. He repays £34. How much does he still owe?

10 The temperature was –3°C before it dropped by 4°C. What is the new temperature?

11 Simon is 2 cm taller than Tony. Terry is 9 cm shorter than Tony. How much taller is Simon than Terry?

12 My train had been running 3 minutes early but stopped for 12 minutes. Is the train now early or late and by how much?

13 Jackie has saved £42. She needs £65. How much more does she need to save?

14 The temperature changed from 3°C to –2°C. Did the temperature rise or fall, and by how much did it change?

15 Neil arrives 5 minutes before his train is due to arrive. The train is 12 minutes late. How long does he have to wait?

16 What year is 15 years before 5 CE?

17 The temperature was 5°C before it dropped by 10°C. What is the new temperature?

18 Hasu owes £102. He repays £55. How much does he still owe?

19 Mary is 2 cm shorter than Paul. Ahsan is 4 cm taller than Paul. How much taller is Ahsan than Mary?

20 Simon misses his bus by 3 minutes. If the buses arrive every 15 minutes, how long does Simon have to wait for the next bus?

Exercise 20B

1 Marsh Hamlet is 17 metres above sea-level and is 22 metres above Marsh End.

How far below sea-level is Marsh End?

2 Camilla arrives 2 minutes after her train is meant to leave but the train is 12 minutes late. How long does Camilla have to wait?

3 Peter is 11 cm taller than Maurice. Naheed is 6 cm taller than Maurice. How much taller is Peter than Naheed?

4 The temperature was –1°C before it rose by 6°C. What is the new temperature?

5 Harry owes the bank £150. He repays £185. How much money does he have in his account now?

6 The temperature changed from 1°C to –4°C. Did the temperature rise or fall, and by how much did it change?

7 My watch is 7 minutes fast. When my watch shows 12.30, what is the correct time?

8 The temperature was 4°C before it dropped by 5°C. What is the new temperature?

9 What year is 18 years before 3 BCE?

10 Jessica owes £11. She earns £34. How much does she have left after she has paid off her debt?

11 The temperature changed from 0°C to –6°C. Did the temperature rise or fall, and by how much did it change?

12 Chris runs a race in 10 seconds less than 4 minutes. Kate is 16 seconds behind Chris. What was Kate's time for the race?

13 What year is 100 years before 5 CE?

14 The temperature was 0°C before it rose by 3°C. What is the new temperature?

15 Sabrina owes £65. She repays £48. How much does she still owe?

16 I arrive 15 minutes before a train is meant to leave but the train leaves 4 minutes early. How long do I have to wait?

17 The temperature changed from –4°C to –2°C. Did the temperature rise or fall, and by how much did it change?

18 Phillip owes £98. He repays £79. How much does he still owe?

19 Olive is 3 cm taller than Sonya. Sumira is 7 cm shorter than Sonya. How much taller is Olive than Sumira?

20 What year is 23 years after 7 BCE?

| + + is replaced by **+** | + − is replaced by **−** |
| − − is replaced by **+** | − + is replaced by **−** |

EXAMPLE
▶ Simplify (+3) − (−2).
− (−2) is replaced by +2.
The calculation is now:
+ 3 + 2 = 5

EXAMPLE
▶ Simplify (+4) − (+3).
− (+3) is replaced by −3.
The calculation is now:
+ 4 − 3 = 1

Exercise 21A

Simplify:

1	(+1) + (−2)	**2**	(+1) + (+3)	**3**	(−4) + (−7)	**4**	(−9) + (+6)
5	(+4) + (−8)	**6**	(+3) + (+7)	**7**	(−11) + (−3)	**8**	0 + (−3)
9	(+15) + (+1)	**10**	(−1) + (+3)	**11**	(+5) + (+2)	**12**	(−16) + (−2)
13	(+6) + (−3)	**14**	(−12) + (−1)	**15**	(−8) + (+4)	**16**	(+14) + (−6)
17	(−21) + (+21)	**18**	0 + (+1)	**19**	(−15) + (+3)	**20**	(−6) + (−6)
21	0 + (−5)	**22**	(−10) + (+1)	**23**	(−20) + (−4)	**24**	(+7) + (+6)
25	(+30) + (−2)	**26**	0 + (−2)	**27**	(+11) + (+7)	**28**	(−12) + (+7)
29	(+3) + (−6)	**30**	(−10) + (−6)				

Exercise 21B

Simplify:

1	(+13) + (+4)	**2**	(−9) + (−9)	**3**	(−3) + (+5)	**4**	(+4) + (+1)
5	(−3) + (−4)	**6**	(−7) + (+2)	**7**	(+9) + (+3)	**8**	(+7) + (−5)
9	(−5) + (+5)	**10**	(+10) + (−1)	**11**	(−6) + (+6)	**12**	(−1) + (−8)
13	(+8) + (−4)	**14**	(+6) + (+4)	**15**	0 + (−2)	**16**	(+10) + (+5)
17	(−5) + (−9)	**18**	(−1) + (+1)	**19**	(+2) + (−4)	**20**	(−3) + (+1)
21	(+11) + (−7)	**22**	0 + (+2)	**23**	(−2) + (+2)	**24**	(+5) + (−1)
25	(−7) + (−3)	**26**	(−4) + (+4)	**27**	0 + (+3)	**28**	(−8) + (+4)
29	(+2) + (+5)	**30**	(−2) + (−6)				

Exercise 21C

Simplify:

1	(+6) − (+5)	**2**	(−4) − (−4)	**3**	(+1) − (−1)	**4**	(−10) − (+2)
5	(+9) − (−3)	**6**	2 − (+3)	**7**	(−2) − (−3)	**8**	(+13) − (−1)
9	(−3) − (−2)	**10**	(+9) − 13	**11**	(−8) − (+8)	**12**	0 − (−3)

13	0 − (+5)	**14**	(−3) − (+2)	**15**	0 − (−5)	**16**	(−2) − (−2)
17	(−1) − 3	**18**	0 − (+7)	**19**	(−4) − (−3)	**20**	(−4) − (+6)
21	(−1) − (−1)	**22**	(+4) − (+2)	**23**	3 − (−2)	**24**	(−7) − 2
25	(+5) − (−1)	**26**	(−7) − (−3)	**27**	0 − (+1)	**28**	(−5) − (+5)
29	(+4) − (−5)	**30**	3 − (+4)				

Exercise 21D

Simplify:

1	(−2) − (+4)	**2**	(−9) − (−1)	**3**	(+8) − (−1)	**4**	(−5) − (−6)
5	0 − (+2)	**6**	14 − (+20)	**7**	(−1) − 1	**8**	(+12) − (−3)
9	(−1) − (−3)	**10**	(−2) − 5	**11**	8 − (+9)	**12**	(−4) − (+5)
13	(−3) − (−3)	**14**	(−6) − (+3)	**15**	(+7) − (−5)	**16**	(−6) − (−2)
17	(+1) − 5	**18**	0 − (−2)	**19**	(−9) − (+8)	**20**	12 − (+15)
21	(−8) − (−5)	**22**	(+2) − (−3)	**23**	(+5) − 4	**24**	(+6) − (−6)
25	(−10) − (−2)	**26**	(−6) − (+7)	**27**	11 − (+8)	**28**	(+10) − (−10)
29	(−4) − (−5)	**30**	(−3) − (+3)				

22/ DIRECTED NUMBERS: MULTIPLICATION AND DIVISION

+ and + gives **+**   + and − gives **−**

− and − gives **+**   − and + gives **−**

The rule is: LIKE SIGNS   give +

UNLIKE SIGNS   give −

EXAMPLES

▶   (+3) × (−5) = −15   (3 × 5 = 15; unlike signs give a minus sign)

(−8) ÷ (−2) = +4 or just 4   (8 ÷ 4 = 2; like signs give a plus sign)

Exercise 22A

1	(+2) × (+4)	**2**	(+4) × (−2)	**3**	(−3) × (−3)	**4**	(−1) × (+2)
5	(+3) × (−4)	**6**	(+1) × (+3)	**7**	(−5) × (−1)	**8**	(−2) × 0
9	0 × (−8)	**10**	(+6) × (−3)	**11**	(+3) × (+5)	**12**	(−1) × (−5)
13	(+1) × (−9)	**14**	(−10) × (+3)	**15**	(+4) × (+2)	**16**	(+4) × (−6)
17	(−5) × 0	**18**	(−6) × (+4)	**19**	(−5) × (+3)	**20**	(+2) × (−1)
21	(−2) × (−4)	**22**	5 × (+6)	**23**	(+2) × (−5)	**24**	(−6) × (+3)
25	(−6) × (−5)	**26**	(+4) × (+3)	**27**	(+7) × (−3)	**28**	(−3) × 10
29	(−7) × (−3)	**30**	(−7) × (+7)				

Exercise 22B

1 $(+5) \times (-3)$	**2** $(+5) \times (+3)$	**3** $(-4) \times (-2)$	**4** $(+6) \times (+5)$
5 $(+10) \times (-4)$	**6** $(-11) \times (-2)$	**7** $(+2) \times (+8)$	**8** $(-5) \times (+5)$
9 $(+1) \times (+8)$	**10** $(-2) \times (+4)$	**11** $(+3) \times (+2)$	**12** $(-6) \times (-2)$
13 $(+8) \times (-2)$	**14** $(-3) \times (+2)$	**15** $6 \times (-2)$	**16** $(-1) \times (-5)$
17 $(+7) \times (+2)$	**18** $(-1) \times (+8)$	**19** $(-4) \times (-3)$	**20** $(+8) \times (-2)$
21 $0 \times (+7)$	**22** $(-4) \times (+7)$	**23** $(-2) \times (-6)$	**24** $(-3) \times (+1)$
25 $(+8) \times (+3)$	**26** $(-3) \times (-4)$	**27** $(+1) \times 0$	**28** $(-4) \times 5$
29 $(+6) \times (+4)$	**30** $(+3) \times (-7)$		

Exercise 22C

1 $(+4) \div (+2)$	**2** $(+9) \div (-3)$	**3** $(-6) \div (+2)$	**4** $(+7) \div (-7)$
5 $(-30) \div 6$	**6** $(+21) \div (-3)$	**7** $(+3) \div (+1)$	**8** $(+10) \div (-2)$
9 $(-40) \div (+5)$	**10** $(+15) \div (+3)$	**11** $(+9) \div (-3)$	**12** $(+18) \div (-3)$
13 $(+24) \div (-8)$	**14** $(+16) \div (+4)$	**15** $(-36) \div (+9)$	**16** $(+5) \div (-1)$
17 $(+2) \div (-2)$	**18** $(+28) \div (+7)$	**19** $(+12) \div (-2)$	**20** $(-49) \div 7$
21 $(+14) \div (+7)$	**22** $(+6) \div (-2)$	**23** $(-8) \div (+2)$	**24** $(+4) \div (-2)$
25 $(+4) \div (-2)$	**26** $(+8) \div (+4)$	**27** $(-12) \div (+3)$	**28** $(+16) \div (-4)$
29 $(+15) \div (-5)$	**30** $(-35) \div (+7)$		

Exercise 22D

1 $(+10) \div (+2)$	**2** $(+12) \div (-6)$	**3** $(+24) \div (-6)$	**4** $(+18) \div (+6)$
5 $(-16) \div (+4)$	**6** $(+18) \div (-3)$	**7** $(+24) \div 4$	**8** $(+30) \div (-6)$
9 $(-20) \div (+10)$	**10** $(+25) \div (-5)$	**11** $(+8) \div (-2)$	**12** $(+10) \div (-5)$
13 $(+9) \div (+3)$	**14** $(-15) \div (+5)$	**15** $(+6) \div (+3)$	**16** $(+8) \div (-2)$
17 $(+6) \div (-3)$	**18** $(-10) \div (+5)$	**19** $(+12) \div (+4)$	**20** $(-32) \div 8$
21 $(+16) \div (-2)$	**22** $(+20) \div (-10)$	**23** $(-18) \div (+9)$	**24** $(+22) \div (-2)$
25 $(+20) \div (+5)$	**26** $(+14) \div (-7)$	**27** $(-33) \div (+11)$	**28** $(+22) \div (+11)$
29 $(+25) \div (-5)$	**30** $(+21) \div (-7)$		

23/ DIRECTED NUMBERS: MIXED EXAMPLES

Exercise 23A

1 $(-7) + (-3)$	**2** $(+30) \div (-6)$	**3** $0 - (+4)$	**4** $(+3) \times (-5)$
5 $(-1) + (-5)$	**6** $(+3) - (-5)$	**7** $(-21) \div (-7)$	**8** $(-4) + (-2)$
9 $(-3) \times (-2)$	**10** $(+6) - (-6)$	**11** $(+10) \div (-2)$	**12** $(+4) + (+5)$
13 $(-4) \times (+2)$	**14** $(-3) - (-1)$	**15** $(-3) \times (-3)$	**16** $(+8) - (+9)$
17 $(+35) \div (-5)$	**18** $(+2) \times (-3)$	**19** $(+9) + (-8)$	**20** $(-4) \times (-5)$

21 $(-32) \div (-8)$	**22** $(+8) + (+5)$	**23** $(-2) \times (-2)$	**24** $(+1) - (+7)$
25 $(-15) \div (+5)$	**26** $(-3) + (-1)$	**27** $(+5) \times (-4)$	**28** $(+24) \div (-6)$
29 $(-3) \times (+4)$	**30** $(+5) - (+7)$		

Exercise 23B

1 $(-2) + (+8)$	**2** $(-1) - (+2)$	**3** $(+3) \times (+6)$	**4** $(-24) \div (-4)$
5 $(-9) + (+6)$	**6** $(-6) - (+6)$	**7** $(+4) \times (+5)$	**8** $(-18) \div (+3)$
9 $(-5) - (-6)$	**10** $(+6) + (-4)$	**11** $(-6) \div (-2)$	**12** $(-4) - (-2)$
13 $(+1) + (-1)$	**14** $(-5) \times (+2)$	**15** $(+4) - (+5)$	**16** $(-8) \div (+4)$
17 $(-2) - (-3)$	**18** $(+3) + (-6)$	**19** $(-3) \times (+2)$	**20** $(+5) + (-4)$
21 $(-9) \div (-3)$	**22** $(-1) \times (-1)$	**23** $(+2) + (+7)$	**24** $(+6) \div (-2)$
25 $(+2) - (+3)$	**26** $(+4) \times (-5)$	**27** $(-5) + (+3)$	**28** $(+18) \div (+3)$
29 $0 - (-1)$	**30** $(+12) \div (-3)$		

24/ RECOGNISING SIMPLE FRACTIONS

EXAMPLE

▶ What fraction is shaded in the diagram?

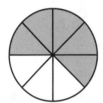

The shape is divided into eight equal portions; each is called $\frac{1}{8}$.

Five of these are shaded and so the fraction that is shaded is $\frac{5}{8}$.

Exercise 24A

There are 20 numbered, shaded areas. State what fraction each area is of the whole shape.

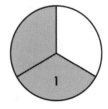

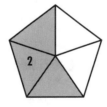

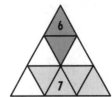

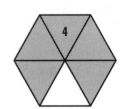

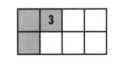

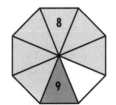

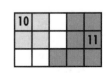

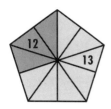
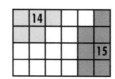

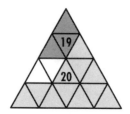

Exercise 24B

There are 20 numbered, shaded areas. State what fraction each area is of the whole shape.

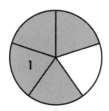

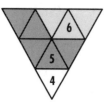

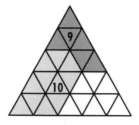
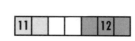

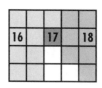

25/ DRAWING SIMPLE FRACTIONS

EXAMPLE

▶ Draw a diagram to show the fraction $\frac{3}{4}$ as part of a circle.

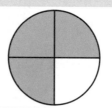

Exercise 25A

Draw a diagram to show each of the following fractions. Use the shape indicated in brackets.

1 $\frac{1}{2}$ (circle) **2** $\frac{2}{5}$ (rectangle) **3** $\frac{2}{3}$ (rectangle) **4** $\frac{1}{6}$ (circle)

5 $\frac{7}{10}$ (rectangle) **6** $\frac{4}{5}$ (circle) **7** $\frac{3}{4}$ (square) **8** $\frac{5}{8}$ (circle)

9 $\frac{7}{16}$ (square)   **10** $\frac{5}{6}$ (rectangle)   **11** $\frac{1}{12}$ and $\frac{5}{12}$ on same diagram (circle)

12 $\frac{4}{15}$ and $\frac{11}{15}$ on same diagram (rectangle)   **13** $\frac{3}{10}$ and $\frac{2}{5}$ on same diagram (rectangle)

14 $\frac{7}{24}$ and $\frac{5}{8}$ on same diagram (rectangle)   **15** $\frac{11}{18}$ and $\frac{1}{3}$ on same diagram (rectangle)

Exercise 25B

Draw a diagram to show each of the following fractions. Use the shape indicated in brackets.

1 $\frac{1}{4}$ (square)   **2** $\frac{3}{5}$ (circle)   **3** $\frac{3}{8}$ (rectangle)   **4** $\frac{2}{9}$ (square)

5 $\frac{5}{16}$ (square)   **6** $\frac{1}{3}$ (circle)   **7** $\frac{9}{10}$ (rectangle)   **8** $\frac{5}{9}$ (square)

9 $\frac{1}{16}$ (rectangle)   **10** $\frac{7}{8}$ (circle)   **11** $\frac{5}{16}$ and $\frac{3}{16}$ on same diagram (square)

12 $\frac{3}{10}$ and $\frac{7}{10}$ on same diagram (rectangle)   **13** $\frac{1}{3}$ and $\frac{1}{6}$ on same diagram (circle)

14 $\frac{9}{20}$ and $\frac{1}{2}$ on same diagram (rectangle)   **15** $\frac{5}{12}$ and $\frac{1}{4}$ on same diagram (rectangle)

26/ EQUIVALENT FRACTIONS

As you can see in the diagrams $\frac{2}{3}$ and $\frac{6}{9}$ are different ways of representing the same thing.

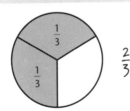

The fractions $\frac{2}{3}$ and $\frac{6}{9}$ are **equivalent** fractions.

The fraction $\frac{6}{9}$ can be cancelled down to $\frac{2}{3}$ by dividing both the top and bottom line by 3.

EXAMPLE

▶ Complete the following by filling in the missing numbers: $\frac{2}{5} = \frac{4}{10} = \frac{6}{?} = \frac{?}{40} = \frac{20}{?}$

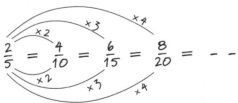

The diagram shows some of the answers: $\frac{2}{5} = \frac{4}{10} = \frac{6}{15} = \frac{16}{40} = \frac{20}{50}$

Exercise 26A

Copy and complete the following.

1 $\frac{3}{4} = \frac{?}{8} = \frac{9}{?} = \frac{?}{32}$

2 $\frac{?}{2} = \frac{2}{4} = \frac{3}{?} = \frac{?}{10}$

3 $\frac{2}{7} = \frac{4}{?} = \frac{6}{?} = \frac{?}{49}$

4 $\frac{1}{16} = \frac{?}{32} = \frac{?}{48} = \frac{5}{?}$

5 $\frac{4}{9} = \frac{8}{?} = \frac{?}{27} = \frac{20}{?}$

6 $\frac{1}{?} = \frac{?}{60} = \frac{3}{90} = \frac{4}{?} = \frac{?}{300}$

7 $\frac{?}{18} = \frac{10}{36} = \frac{20}{?} = \frac{30}{?} = \frac{?}{144}$

8 $\frac{11}{12} = \frac{22}{?} = \frac{?}{48} = \frac{55}{?} = \frac{77}{?}$

9 $\frac{2}{?} = \frac{?}{50} = \frac{?}{100} = \frac{16}{200} = \frac{?}{250}$

10 $\frac{7}{24} = \frac{14}{?} = \frac{?}{72} = \frac{28}{?} = \frac{?}{144}$

Exercise 26B

Copy and complete the following.

1 $\frac{2}{3} = \frac{4}{?} = \frac{?}{12} = \frac{12}{?}$

2 $\frac{?}{6} = \frac{2}{12} = \frac{3}{?} = \frac{?}{24}$

3 $\frac{3}{?} = \frac{6}{10} = \frac{12}{?} = \frac{?}{25}$

4 $\frac{2}{15} = \frac{?}{30} = \frac{6}{?} = \frac{?}{90}$

5 $\frac{5}{?} = \frac{?}{16} = \frac{15}{24} = \frac{25}{?}$

6 $\frac{?}{10} = \frac{?}{20} = \frac{9}{?} = \frac{?}{80} = \frac{30}{100}$

7 $\frac{5}{36} = \frac{10}{?} = \frac{?}{108} = \frac{20}{?} = \frac{?}{216}$

8 $\frac{11}{20} = \frac{22}{?} = \frac{33}{?} = \frac{?}{80} = \frac{?}{120}$

9 $\frac{9}{?} = \frac{18}{100} = \frac{27}{?} = \frac{36}{?} = \frac{?}{450}$

10 $\frac{?}{32} = \frac{30}{64} = \frac{?}{96} = \frac{60}{?} = \frac{120}{?}$

27/ FRACTIONS OF QUANTITIES

EXAMPLE

▶ Find $\frac{1}{3}$ of 72.

$\frac{1}{3}$ of 72 = 72 ÷ 3
= 24

EXAMPLE

▶ Find $\frac{3}{10}$ of £4.50.

$\frac{1}{10}$ of £4.50 = £4.50 ÷ 10
= £0.45 or 45p

$\frac{3}{10}$ of £4.50 = £0.45 × 3
= £1.35

Exercise 27A

1 $\frac{1}{2}$ of £15

2 $\frac{1}{4}$ of 24 kg

3 $\frac{1}{3}$ of 57 mm

4 $\frac{1}{9}$ of 36p

5 $\frac{1}{9}$ of £36

6 $\frac{1}{100}$ of £6

7 $\frac{1}{8}$ of £56

8 $\frac{1}{7}$ of 42

9 $\frac{1}{6}$ of 24p

10 $\frac{1}{20}$ of 80

11 $\frac{1}{3}$ of 72 km

12 $\frac{1}{15}$ of $60

13 $\frac{1}{4}$ of £3

14 $\frac{1}{5}$ of 30 mm

15 $\frac{1}{8}$ of £4

16 $\frac{1}{10}$ of 60

17 $\frac{1}{5}$ of 80 kg

18 $\frac{1}{6}$ of £9

19 $\frac{1}{25}$ of 50 litres

20 $\frac{1}{12}$ of £42

Exercise 27B

1 $\frac{1}{3}$ of 12 kg   **2** $\frac{1}{4}$ of 48 mm   **3** $\frac{1}{2}$ of £7   **4** $\frac{1}{12}$ of 96   **5** $\frac{1}{8}$ of £24

6 $\frac{1}{3}$ of 84 g   **7** $\frac{1}{15}$ of 75   **8** $\frac{1}{7}$ of 14 km   **9** $\frac{1}{8}$ of 16 litres   **10** $\frac{1}{4}$ of £10

11 $\frac{1}{6}$ of 30 m   **12** $\frac{1}{5}$ of 25 g   **13** $\frac{1}{2}$ of £1.12   **14** $\frac{1}{7}$ of £35   **15** $\frac{1}{5}$ of 45 g

16 $\frac{1}{10}$ of 50 kg   **17** $\frac{1}{20}$ of £40   **18** $\frac{1}{10}$ of £3   **19** $\frac{1}{50}$ of £250   **20** $\frac{1}{100}$ of £5

Exercise 27C

1 $\frac{3}{5}$ of 15 cm   **2** $\frac{2}{3}$ of 12 km   **3** $\frac{5}{6}$ of 42 cm   **4** $\frac{3}{8}$ of 64   **5** $\frac{2}{5}$ of £20

6 $\frac{5}{8}$ of 40   **7** $\frac{2}{3}$ of 36 litres   **8** $\frac{7}{8}$ of 72 m   **9** $\frac{4}{5}$ of £20   **10** $\frac{3}{10}$ of 50

11 $\frac{6}{7}$ of 21 m   **12** $\frac{3}{4}$ of 56 litres   **13** $\frac{9}{10}$ of 20 kg   **14** $\frac{3}{20}$ of £60   **15** $\frac{3}{8}$ of 24

16 $\frac{4}{7}$ of 56 kg   **17** $\frac{7}{10}$ of £5   **18** $\frac{3}{4}$ of 64 litres   **19** $\frac{5}{7}$ of 21 kg   **20** $\frac{7}{10}$ of £30

Exercise 27D

1 $\frac{3}{4}$ of 28 m   **2** $\frac{5}{6}$ of £18   **3** $\frac{2}{5}$ of 45   **4** $\frac{2}{3}$ of 45 g   **5** $\frac{6}{7}$ of 35 mm

6 $\frac{3}{5}$ of 55 cm   **7** $\frac{5}{8}$ of £16   **8** $\frac{3}{4}$ of 72 kg   **9** $\frac{2}{9}$ of 18 litres   **10** $\frac{4}{5}$ of 15p

11 $\frac{7}{8}$ of 400   **12** $\frac{2}{3}$ of £36   **13** $\frac{3}{8}$ of 40 m   **14** $\frac{5}{6}$ of £48   **15** $\frac{3}{5}$ of £100

16 $\frac{9}{10}$ of 200 m   **17** $\frac{3}{25}$ of 50 cm   **18** $\frac{5}{9}$ of 27   **19** $\frac{3}{10}$ of £60   **20** $\frac{2}{5}$ of £35

28/ RECOGNISING SIMPLE PERCENTAGES

1% means '1 in every 100'.
If a shape is divided into 100 pieces, then one of those pieces is 1%.

EXAMPLE

▶ What percentage of the diagram is shaded and labelled as P and as Q?

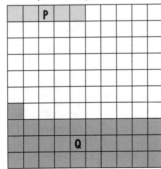

There are 100 squares in the diagram. This means that each square is 1% of the whole.
P is 5 squares and so is 5%.
Q is 31 squares and so is 31%.

Exercise 28A

For each labelled area, state the percentage of the diagram that is shaded.

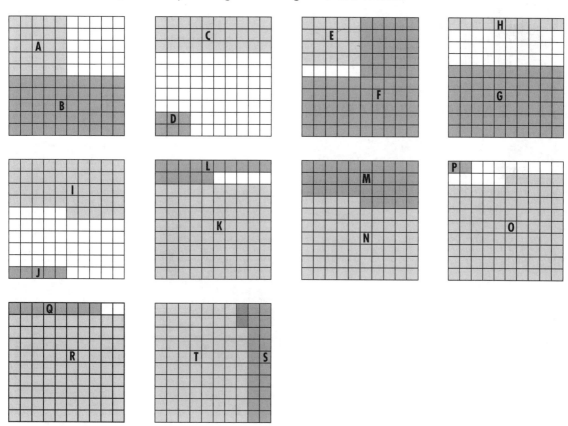

Exercise 28B

For each labelled area, state the percentage of the diagram that is shaded.

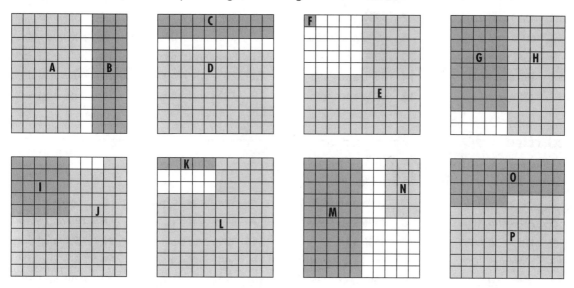

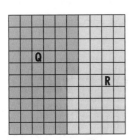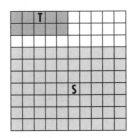

29/ DRAWING SIMPLE PERCENTAGES

EXAMPLE

► Draw a grid with 100 squares.
Shade and label
(a) 20%
(b) 50% of the grid.

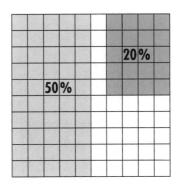

Exercise 29A

Draw a grid with 100 squares as in Exercise 28.
Shade and label the following percentages.

1	45% and 25%	**2**	32% and 18%	**3**	50% and 6%	**4**	75% and 15%
5	60% and 20%	**6**	40% and 35%	**7**	85% and 10%	**8**	8% and 22%
9	95% and 2%	**10**	30% and 56%	**11**	80% and 16%	**12**	70% and 25%
13	1% and 90%	**14**	88% and 12%	**15**	20% and 75%	**16**	40% and 60%
17	45% and 55%	**18**	65% and 35%	**19**	72% and 18%	**20**	42% and 48%

Exercise 29B

Draw a grid with 100 squares as in Exercise 28.
Shade and label the following percentages.

1	2% and 54%	**2**	10% and 60%	**3**	30% and 70%	**4**	50% and 45%
5	25% and 40%	**6**	75% and 15%	**7**	80% and 5%	**8**	1% and 90%
9	12% and 85%	**10**	55% and 35%	**11**	20% and 65%	**12**	35% and 50%
13	13% and 12%	**14**	15% and 75%	**15**	60% and 40%	**16**	78% and 22%
17	56% and 25%	**18**	30% and 20%	**19**	65% and 35%	**20**	87% and 3%

Remember: $\frac{1}{100}$ is 1%.

$\frac{1}{20} = \frac{5}{100}$ (multiply the 20 by 5 to get 100; then multiply the top by 5 as well)

So, $\frac{1}{20} = 5\%$

Here are some useful conversions that you should learn. They will save you time later in life.

$\frac{1}{2} = 50\%$	$\frac{1}{4} = 25\%$	$\frac{1}{10} = 10\%$	$\frac{1}{20} = 5\%$	$\frac{1}{25} = 4\%$
	$\frac{3}{4} = 75\%$	$\frac{3}{10} = 30\%$	$\frac{3}{20} = 15\%$	$\frac{3}{25} = 12\%$
		$\frac{7}{10} = 70\%$	$\frac{7}{20} = 35\%$	$\frac{7}{25} = 28\%$
$\frac{1}{3} = 33\frac{1}{3}\%$	$\frac{1}{5} = 20\%$	$\frac{9}{10} = 90\%$	$\frac{9}{20} = 45\%$	$\frac{9}{25} = 36\%$
$\frac{2}{3} = 66\frac{2}{3}\%$	$\frac{2}{5} = 40\%$		$\frac{11}{20} = 55\%$	
	$\frac{3}{5} = 60\%$		$\frac{13}{20} = 65\%$	$\frac{1}{40} = 2\frac{1}{2}\%$
	$\frac{4}{5} = 80\%$		$\frac{17}{20} = 85\%$	$\frac{1}{50} = 2\%$
			$\frac{19}{20} = 95\%$	$\frac{1}{100} = 1\%$

EXAMPLE

▶ Write $\frac{13}{20}$ as a percentage.

$$\frac{1}{20} = 5\%$$

So $\frac{13}{20} = 13 \times 5\%$

$= 65\%$

Exercise 30A

Convert to percentages.

1 $\frac{1}{5}$ **2** $\frac{3}{10}$ **3** $\frac{1}{2}$ **4** $\frac{1}{3}$ **5** $\frac{1}{4}$

6 $\frac{3}{5}$ **7** $\frac{9}{10}$ **8** $\frac{3}{4}$ **9** $\frac{1}{20}$ **10** $\frac{1}{10}$

11 $\frac{7}{20}$ **12** $\frac{4}{25}$ **13** $\frac{3}{100}$ **14** $\frac{1}{25}$ **15** $\frac{9}{25}$

16 $\frac{3}{20}$ **17** $\frac{7}{10}$ **18** $\frac{66}{100}$ **19** $\frac{2}{3}$ **20** $\frac{3}{50}$

Exercise 30B

Convert to percentages.

1 $\frac{3}{4}$ **2** $\frac{1}{2}$ **3** $\frac{2}{5}$ **4** $\frac{1}{20}$ **5** $\frac{2}{3}$

6 $\frac{3}{4}$ **7** $\frac{2}{25}$ **8** $\frac{1}{4}$ **9** $\frac{1}{5}$ **10** $\frac{1}{3}$

11 $\frac{4}{5}$ **12** $\frac{21}{100}$ **13** $\frac{7}{50}$ **14** $\frac{11}{20}$ **15** $\frac{17}{20}$

16 $\frac{3}{5}$ **17** $\frac{3}{25}$ **18** $\frac{1}{100}$ **19** $\frac{47}{100}$ **20** $\frac{7}{20}$

31/ FRACTIONS TO PERCENTAGES WITH A CALCULATOR

To convert a fraction to a percentage, multiply by 100.

> **EXAMPLE**
>
> ▶ Convert $\frac{4}{5}$ to a percentage.
>
> Press these keys on the calculator: $\boxed{4}$ $\boxed{÷}$ $\boxed{5}$ $\boxed{×}$ $\boxed{100}$ $\boxed{=}$
> This gives an answer of 80%.

Exercise 31A

Convert the following fractions to percentages.

1 $\frac{2}{5}$ **2** $\frac{3}{8}$ **3** $\frac{1}{3}$ **4** $\frac{9}{50}$ **5** $\frac{17}{20}$

6 $\frac{1}{5}$ **7** $\frac{13}{20}$ **8** $\frac{9}{40}$ **9** $\frac{1}{8}$ **10** $\frac{4}{25}$

11 $\frac{2}{9}$ **12** $\frac{6}{25}$ **13** $\frac{1}{9}$ **14** $\frac{9}{25}$ **15** $\frac{7}{8}$

16 $\frac{1}{6}$ **17** $\frac{19}{40}$ **18** $\frac{29}{50}$ **19** $\frac{11}{25}$ **20** $\frac{5}{12}$

Exercise 31B

Convert the following fractions to percentages.

1 $\frac{7}{25}$ **2** $\frac{3}{20}$ **3** $\frac{4}{5}$ **4** $\frac{2}{3}$ **5** $\frac{21}{50}$

6 $\frac{3}{4}$ **7** $\frac{1}{25}$ **8** $\frac{3}{5}$ **9** $\frac{8}{25}$ **10** $\frac{4}{9}$

11 $\frac{5}{8}$ **12** $\frac{21}{25}$ **13** $\frac{19}{20}$ **14** $\frac{5}{6}$ **15** $\frac{18}{25}$

16 $\frac{37}{50}$ **17** $\frac{7}{12}$ **18** $\frac{3}{25}$ **19** $\frac{29}{40}$ **20** $\frac{24}{25}$

32/ PERCENTAGES TO FRACTIONS: SIMPLE CONVERSIONS WITHOUT A CALCULATOR

Remember: 1% means $\frac{1}{100}$ and so 7% = $\frac{7}{100}$ and 13% = $\frac{13}{100}$.

Here are some useful conversions:

1% = $\frac{1}{100}$	15% = $\frac{3}{20}$	40% = $\frac{2}{5}$	65% = $\frac{13}{20}$	90% = $\frac{9}{10}$
2% = $\frac{1}{50}$	20% = $\frac{1}{5}$	45% = $\frac{9}{20}$	70% = $\frac{7}{10}$	95% = $\frac{19}{20}$
4% = $\frac{1}{25}$	25% = $\frac{1}{4}$	50% = $\frac{1}{2}$	75% = $\frac{3}{4}$	100% = 1
5% = $\frac{1}{20}$	30% = $\frac{3}{10}$	55% = $\frac{11}{20}$	80% = $\frac{4}{5}$	$33\frac{1}{3}$% = $\frac{1}{3}$
10% = $\frac{1}{10}$	35% = $\frac{7}{20}$	60% = $\frac{3}{5}$	85% = $\frac{17}{20}$	$66\frac{2}{3}$% = $\frac{2}{3}$

EXAMPLE

▶ Convert 55% to a fraction in its simplest form.

$$55\% = \frac{\overset{11}{\cancel{55}}}{\underset{20}{\cancel{100}}} = \frac{11}{20} \text{ (cancel both the top and bottom by 5)}$$

This was a simple conversion and the answer could have been found by looking at the conversion table above.

EXAMPLE

▶ Convert 24% to a fraction in its simplest form.

$$24\% = \frac{24}{100} = \frac{6}{25} \text{ (cancel both the top and bottom by 4)}$$

Or, 4% = $\frac{1}{25}$ (from the table)

So, 24% = $\frac{6}{25}$

Exercise 32A

Convert the following percentages to fractions.

1	50%	**2**	25%	**3**	1%	**4**	5%	**5**	45%
6	10%	**7**	90%	**8**	7%	**9**	40%	**10**	19%
11	65%	**12**	12%	**13**	$33\frac{1}{3}$%	**14**	22%	**15**	4%
16	100%	**17**	6%	**18**	30%	**19**	34%	**20**	16%

Exercise 32B

Convert the following percentages to fractions.

1	3%	**2**	75%	**3**	2%	**4**	15%	**5**	70%
6	35%	**7**	13%	**8**	8%	**9**	60%	**10**	21%
11	$66\frac{2}{3}$%	**12**	26%	**13**	85%	**14**	17%	**15**	95%
16	80%	**17**	44%	**18**	20%	**19**	24%	**20**	55%

33/ CALCULATING PERCENTAGES OF QUANTITIES WITHOUT A CALCULATOR

There are several tricks that can be used to calculate simple percentages. Here are two of them.

Recognising the fraction

If you recognise the conversion of the percentage into a fraction, then the calculation is much easier.

> **EXAMPLE**
>
> ▶ Find 75% of 32 kg.
>
> $$75\% = \frac{3}{4}$$
>
> $$\frac{1}{4} \text{ of } 32 \text{ kg} = 8 \text{ kg}$$
>
> Therefore $\frac{3}{4}$ of 32 kg = 3 × 8 kg = 24 kg

Using that 1% of £1 is 1p

Knowing that 1% of £1 = 1p allows you to say that 3% of £1 = 3p etc.

> **EXAMPLE**
>
> ▶ Find 7% of £5
>
> $$7\% \text{ of } £5 = 5 \times 7\text{p}$$
> $$= 35\text{p}$$

Exercise 33A

Find the following:

1 10% of 50 m	**2** 25% of £24	**3** 50% of 36 cm	**4** $33\frac{1}{3}$% of £30
5 3% of £2	**6** 11% of £4	**7** 75% of 8 km	**8** 5% of 40
9 7% of £5	**10** 6% of £7	**11** 20% of 50 g	**12** 2% of £5
13 13% of £10	**14** $66\frac{2}{3}$% of 24 mm	**15** 60% of 50	**16** 9% of £4
17 40% of 10 ml	**18** 4% of £6	**19** 30% of £2	**20** 80% of £15

Exercise 33B

Find the following:

1 1% of £7	**2** 50% of 16 kg	**3** 3% of £6	**4** 20% of 30
5 75% of 20 km	**6** 7% of £2	**7** $33\frac{1}{3}$% of £60	**8** 11% of £5
9 25% of 80	**10** 8% of £4	**11** 5% of £20	**12** 10% of 40
13 40% of 30 g	**14** 9% of £2	**15** $66\frac{2}{3}$% of 18	**16** 60% of £10
17 2% of £15	**18** 80% of 15	**19** 17% of £2	**20** 30% of 50

34/ CALCULATING PERCENTAGES OF QUANTITIES WITH A CALCULATOR

To calculate 1% of a quantity, simply multiply by $\frac{1}{100}$.

To calculate 3% of a quantity, simply multiply by $\frac{3}{100}$.
This is $\boxed{\times 3}$ followed by $\boxed{\div 100}$.

> **EXAMPLE**
> ▶ Find 17% of £13.40.
>
> 17% of £13.40 $= £13.40 \times \frac{17}{100}$ (calculator: $\boxed{13.40}$ $\boxed{\times}$ $\boxed{17}$ $\boxed{\div}$ $\boxed{100}$ $\boxed{=}$)
>
> $= £2.278$ (calculator answer)
>
> $= £2.28$ (to the nearest 1p)
>
> (Note: The answer is nearer to £2.28 than £2.27.)

Exercise 34A

Calculate the following using a calculator.

1 9% of £46
2 6% of 450
3 12% of 560 kg
4 7% of £120
5 5% of £65
6 8% of 17 m
7 14% of 450
8 24% of £25
9 16% of 150 ml
10 19% of £27
11 7% of 112 m
12 22% of 7.5 km
13 14% of 14 kg
14 11% of £165
15 4% of 68
16 5% of 60 g
17 13% of £32
18 21% of 350
19 17% of 160 km
20 23% of 660

Exercise 34B

Calculate the following using a calculator.

1 7% of £45
2 3% of £63
3 2% of 157
4 4% of £21.75
5 8% of 23.9 km
6 9% of 84 m
7 6% of £140
8 11% of 540 km
9 9% of 225
10 13% of £650
11 16% of 230 kg
12 6% of 45 g
13 21% of £67
14 15% of 150
15 35% of 360 m
16 24% of 175 kg
17 13% of £131
18 12% of 360
19 35% of £13.80
20 14% of £620

35/ PROBLEMS INVOLVING SIMPLE PERCENTAGES OF QUANTITIES

Remember: Show your calculations so that it is clear that you know what you are doing.

> **EXAMPLE**
>
> ▶ A certain metal contains 30% tin. What is the weight of tin in 150 g of metal?
>
> $$30\% \text{ of } 150 \text{ g} = \frac{30}{100} \times 150 \text{ g}$$
> $$= 45 \text{ g}$$

Exercise 35A

1 There are 40 people at a meeting. Of these, 30% of them voted for Claire. How many votes did she receive?

2 If 25% of the 76 fish in a pond are goldfish, how many goldfish are there?

3 Chips cost 70p a portion but the price is increased by 20%. What is the increase in the price of a portion of chips?

4 A 750-ml bottle of a fruit drink contains 40% orange juice. How much orange juice is there in the bottle?

5 Neil wins £125 but has to pay 9% in tax. How much tax does he have to pay?

6 Mansoora has 120 tiles but find she needs another 30%. How many more tiles does she need?

7 The price of a pair of shoes is reduced by 20%. If the original price is £37, how much is the reduction?

8 At a school of 1750 pupils exactly 2% are absent on a particular day. How many are absent?

9 Brass contains 34% zinc. How much zinc is their in 450 grams of zinc?

10 If prices are increased by 3%, what is the increase on a chair that used to cost £52?

11 A driver receives a no-claim bonus of 60% on his insurance. How much is his no-claim bonus on insurance costing £480?

12 A margarine contains 80% fat. How much fat is there in 250 grams of margarine?

13 As part of his exercise programme a jogger decides to increase his distance run per week by 40%. If he runs 35 km per week, how much extra must he run?

14 A screenwash contains 25% antifreeze. How much antifreeze is there in 600 ml of screenwash?

15 The price of a holiday is reduced by 15%. What is the reduction on a holiday costing £360?

16 Tax of 45% is charged on £240. How much is the tax?

Exercise 35B

1 Alice scores 60% of the maximum 40 marks in an examination. What is her mark?

2 If 28% of 150 mice delivered to a pet store were white, how many mice were not white?

3 The label on a can states that it contains '25% extra FREE'. How much extra is there in a can that normally contains 440 ml?

4 Mark receives a pay rise of 3%. If he earns £156.60 per week, how much is his pay rise to the nearest penny?

5 The average rainfall in Melbourne is 650 mm per year. How much extra rain will fall if this increases by 8%?

6 Everything is reduced by 15% in a sale. How much is the reduction on a coat priced at £92?

7 The petrol tank on a car holds 56 litres. The latest model of the car has a tank that holds 15% more than this. How much extra petrol will it hold?

8 The price of a holiday costing £399 is increased by 5%. How much is the extra cost?

9 A certain metal contains 7.5% lead. How much lead is there in 224 grams of metal?

10 A brand of instant potato contains 91% potato. How much of 120 grams of instant potato is *not* potato?

11 A factory making 2500 tables a week needs to increase production by 36%. How many extra tables is this?

12 Bhaveen calculates that 42% of his earnings are deducted each week. How much are the deductions if he earns £216 per week?

13 If 30% of a town of 225 000 people are aged over 65, how many are aged over 65?

14 A packet of breakfast cereal normally contains 480 grams. How much extra is there in a packet which contains $12\frac{1}{2}$% extra?

15 A savings account gives 6% interest in a year. How much is the interest on £760?

16 A company is reducing their prices by 8% for customers who pay within a month. How much is the reduction on £3500?

36/ IDENTIFYING TYPES OF NUMBER

Here are some examples of ways of describing types of number.

Multiples of 3: Numbers that are obtained by multiplying by 3, for example, 3, 6, 9, 12, ...

Factors of 36: Numbers that divide exactly into 36; these are 1, 2, 3, 4, 6, 9, 12, 18 and 36.

Prime numbers: Numbers that can be divided only by 1 and the number itself, for example, 2, 3, 5, 7, 11, 13 ... . (Note: 1 is not a prime number.)

Squares: A number that is obtained by multiplying a number by itself, for example, 1, 4, 9, 16, 25, 36 ... .

EXAMPLE

▶ 22, 9, 17, 16, 35, 27

Select the number from the list that is described by the words. You can use each number *once* only.

(a) A prime number (b) A multiple of 9 (c) A square number
(d) A multiple of 11 (e) A factor of 36 (f) An odd number

17 is the only prime number.
9 and 27 are multiples of 9.
9 and 16 are both square numbers.
22 is the only multiple of 11.
9 is the only factor of 36.
9, 17, 27 and 35 are odd numbers.
So, the only way that the numbers can be selected is:
(a) 17 (b) 27 (c) 16 (d) 22 (e) 9 (f) 35

Exercise 36A

1 Which of the following numbers is a multiple of 3?
23, 17, 18, 5, 19, 20

2 Which of the following numbers is a prime number?
12, 13, 14, 15, 16, 18

3 Which of the following numbers are factors of 75?
25, 35, 45, 55, 5, 15, 37

4 Which of the following numbers are square numbers?
24, 36, 48, 64, 15, 28, 1

5 Which of the following numbers are prime numbers?
9, 15, 21, 27, 35, 42, 49, 55

6 8, 14, 35, 36, 4, 19, 12, 31
There are two examples of each of the following in the above list. Name them.
(a) Factors of 24   (b) Multiples of 7   (c) Square numbers   (d) Prime numbers

7 9, 11, 23, 32, 45, 49, 15, 8
There are two examples of each of the following in the above list. Name them.
(a) Multiples of 5   (b) Factors of 32   (c) Prime numbers   (d) Square numbers

8 1, 27, 12, 10, 20, 64, 13, 29
There are two examples of each of the following in the above list. Name them.
(a) Factors of 100   (b) Multiples of 3   (c) Square numbers   (d) Prime numbers

9 81, 12, 7, 10, 18, 37, 20, 16
There are two examples of each of the following in the above list. Name them.
(a) Square numbers   (b) Multiples of 6   (c) Prime numbers   (d) Factors of 40

10 121, 21, 25, 14, 17, 24, 5, 8
There are two examples of each of the following in the above list. Name them.
(a) Factors of 84   (b) Square numbers   (c) Multiples of 4   (d) Prime numbers

11 5, 18, 21, 29, 16, 8
Give *one* example of each of the following from the list of numbers. Use each number *once* only.
(a) A factor of 24   (b) A prime number   (c) An odd number
(d) A factor of 15   (e) A multiple of 9   (f) A square number

12 10, 13, 14, 15, 21, 25
Give *one* example of each of the following from the list of numbers. Use each number *once* only.
(a) A factor of 40   (b) A multiple of 7   (c) An even number
(d) A prime number   (e) A multiple of 5   (f) A square number

Exercise 36B

1 Which of the following numbers is a multiple of 5?
11, 12, 13, 14, 15, 16

2 Which of the following numbers is a factor of 32?
5, 6, 7, 8, 10, 12

3 Which of the following numbers are prime numbers?
28, 29, 31, 33, 35, 37, 39

4 Which of the following numbers are square numbers?
5, 9, 12, 16, 18, 22, 25, 35

5 Which of the following numbers are factors of 48?
6, 8, 9, 12, 18, 24, 16, 30

6 53, 6, 169, 13, 24, 18, 49, 8
There are two examples of each of the following in the above list. Name them.
(a) Factors of 36   (b) Multiples of 4   (c) Square numbers   (d) Prime numbers

7 25, 15, 23, 4, 21, 64, 19, 8
There are two examples of each of the following in the above list. Name them.
(a) Square numbers (b) Multiples of 3 (c) Prime numbers (d) Factors of 56

8 31, 50, 36, 8, 81, 29, 4, 20
There are two examples of each of the following in the above list. Name them.
(a) Factors of 32 (b) Multiples of 10 (c) Square numbers (d) Prime numbers

9 36, 21, 23, 28, 100, 12, 20, 17
There are two examples of each of the following in the above list. Name them.
(a) Multiples of 7 (b) Factors of 60 (c) Square numbers (d) Prime numbers

10 18, 27, 29, 16, 61, 6, 49, 8
There are two examples of each of the following in the above list. Name them.
(a) Factors of 24 (b) Square numbers (c) Multiples of 9 (d) Prime numbers

11 100, 25, 39, 31, 30, 18
Give *one* example of each of the following from the list of numbers. Use each number *once* only.
(a) A multiple of 5 (b) A prime number (c) An odd number
(d) A factor of 50 (e) A multiple of 6 (f) A square number

12 18, 5, 6, 3, 81, 20
Give *one* example of each of the following from the list of numbers. Use each number *once* only.
(a) A factor of 27 (b) A multiple of 9 (c) An even number
(d) A prime number (e) A multiple of 4 (f) A square number

REVISION

Exercise B

1 Rewrite the following in ascending order: −7, 0, 5, −1, −5.

2 (a) (−3) × (+2) (b) (−5) + (−4) (c) (−3) − (−5) (d) (+1) ÷ (−1)

3 Draw a circle and shade $\frac{3}{8}$ of it.

4 Draw a rectangle; shade $\frac{3}{5}$ and $\frac{3}{10}$ of it. Label the areas to show which is which.

5 State the fraction of the square that is shaded. What fraction is unshaded?

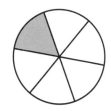

6 State the fraction of the circle that is shaded. What fraction is unshaded?

7 Copy and complete the following:

$$\frac{2}{3} = \frac{?}{6} = \frac{6}{9} = \frac{?}{21}$$

8 State the percentage of the diagram that is labelled A and the percentage that is labelled B. What percentage of the diagram remains unshaded?

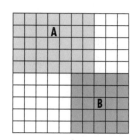

9 Draw a 10 × 10 grid similar to the one in question 8. Shade and label 75% and 15% of it. What percentage remains unshaded?

10 Convert the following to percentages.

    (a) $\frac{3}{4}$ (b) $\frac{1}{2}$ (c) $\frac{2}{5}$ (d) $\frac{3}{10}$

11 Convert the following to fractions, cancelling down to their simplest form.

    (a) 25%   (b) 60%   (c) 5%   (d) 20%

12 Find the following:

    (a) $\frac{1}{8}$ of 72 kg   (b) $\frac{1}{5}$ of £45   (c) $\frac{2}{3}$ of 600   (d) $\frac{3}{10}$ of £25

13 Find the following:

    (a) 3% of £5   (b) 5% of 200   (c) 80% of 50   (d) 25% of 120

14 8, 20, 24, 25, 29, 53, 60, 64

There are two examples of each of the following in the above list. Name them.

    (a) Multiples of 12   (b) Factors of 80   (c) Prime numbers   (d) Square numbers

Exercise BB

1 What year is 20 years after 5 BCE? (Note: BCE ≡ BC and CE ≡ AD.)

2 The temperature was −7°C but is now −16°C. Has the temperature risen or fallen, and by how much?

3 Graham's train is 30 minutes late but he arrives 3 minutes after the train's proper arrival time. How long does he have to wait?

4 Bhaldip has £95 in his bank account. He writes a cheque for £120. How much does he owe now?

5 If $\frac{2}{7}$ of a class of 28 are absent, how many students remain?

6 If $\frac{3}{4}$ of the cost of making a dress is materials, what is the price of the materials for a dress that costs £48 to make?

7 What is the cost of $2\frac{1}{2}$ kg of apples at 96p per kg?

8 Simon saves $\frac{3}{8}$ of his money and spends the rest. What fraction does he spend? If he earns £24, how much does he save?

9 Cathy owes £75 but manages to pay off 60% of it. How much did she pay off and what percentage does she still owe?

10 A piece of brass weighing 120 grams contains 55% copper. What is the weight of copper that it contains?

11 A biscuit contains 8% fat. What weight of fat is there in 60 grams of the biscuits?

12 The price of an exercise bicycle is reduced by 30% in a sale. If the price was £156, what is its price in the sale?

13 32, 9, 36, 7, 14, 15

Give *one* example of each of the following from the list of numbers. Use each number *once* only.

    (a) A factor of 64   (b) A multiple of 7   (c) An odd number

    (d) A prime number   (e) A factor of 54   (f) A square number

Algebra

37/ SIMPLE EQUATIONS

$\square + 5 = 8$ is a type of **equation.** It can only be true if $\square$ is given the value of 3.

EXAMPLE

▶ $\square - 7 = 2$

$\square$ has the value 9 or, this can be written, $\square = 9$.

Exercise 37A

In each of the following, find a value for $\square$.

1 $3 + \square = 7$	**2** $2 \times \square = 14$	**3** $\square + 2 = 8$	**4** $\square \div 5 = 3$
5 $\square - 5 = 2$	**6** $\square \times 4 = 20$	**7** $11 - \square = 8$	**8** $18 \div \square = 6$
9 $6 \times \square = 24$	**10** $\square + 1 = 10$	**11** $\square \times 4 = 28$	**12** $\square \div 5 = 6$
13 $\square + 3 = 9$	**14** $32 \div \square = 8$	**15** $\square - 7 = 5$	**16** $\square \times 6 = 42$
17 $\square \div 2 = 9$	**18** $5 + \square = 5$	**19** $\square \times 2 = 20$	**20** $\square - 4 = 4$
21 $4 + \square = 7$	**22** $15 \div \square = 5$	**23** $\square \times 8 = 64$	**24** $\square - 1 = 4$
25 $\square - 1 = 8$	**26** $8 + \square = 13$	**27** $13 + \square = 15$	**28** $24 \div \square = 3$
29 $\square \times 3 = 21$	**30** $10 - \square = 6$		

Exercise 37B

In each of the following, find a value for $\square$.

1 $\square - 12 = 5$	**2** $\square + 18 = 21$	**3** $\square \times 6 = 36$	**4** $40 \div \square = 5$
5 $1 + \square = 10$	**6** $8 - \square = 3$	**7** $2 \times \square = 12$	**8** $\square \div 4 = 7$
9 $35 \div \square = 7$	**10** $9 + \square = 17$	**11** $12 - \square = 7$	**12** $\square \times 2 = 6$
13 $\square \times 3 = 18$	**14** $\square + 3 = 16$	**15** $15 - \square = 13$	**16** $\square \div 4 = 5$
17 $6 + \square = 15$	**18** $\square \div 7 = 6$	**19** $\square + 7 = 24$	**20** $8 + \square = 11$
21 $\square \div 5 = 9$	**22** $\square \times 4 = 16$	**23** $8 \times \square = 16$	**24** $\square + 8 = 10$
25 $5 \times \square = 30$	**26** $14 - \square = 2$	**27** $21 - \square = 5$	**28** $\square - 3 = 8$
29 $36 \div \square = 9$	**30** $7 \times \square = 49$		

To solve equations, collect the numbers on one side of the equation and the unknowns on the other side.

This can be done by adding or subtracting from both sides: this can be expressed as the simple rule, 'Cross the bridge and change the sign'.

EXAMPLE

▶ $x + 3 = 9$

This means that $x = 9 - 3$
$x = 6$

When a term is moved from one side of the equation to the other, the sign of that term is changed.

EXAMPLE

▶ $10 - x = 3$

$10 - 3 = x$
$7 = x$
$x = 7$

Exercise 38A

Solve the equations.

1 $x + 3 = 5$	**2** $5 + x = 8$	**3** $x - 2 = 3$	**4** $x + 1 = 4$
5 $x - 6 = 2$	**6** $x + 4 = 5$	**7** $x + 8 = 12$	**8** $x - 20 = 5$
9 $x + 6 = 10$	**10** $x - 9 = 2$	**11** $x - 5 = 4$	**12** $x + 2 = 5$
13 $x + 7 = 8$	**14** $x - 4 = 2$	**15** $3 + x = 7$	**16** $x + 9 = 11$
17 $x - 8 = 4$	**18** $x - 4 = 9$	**19** $x - 1 = 7$	**20** $1 + x = 3$
21 $x + 2 = 9$	**22** $7 - x = 5$	**23** $x + 4 = 9$	**24** $1 - x = 0$
25 $x - 6 = 3$	**26** $5 - x = 1$	**27** $3 - x = 1$	**28** $x + 15 = 20$
29 $9 - x = 5$	**30** $15 - x = 8$		

Exercise 38B

Solve the equations.

1 $x + 2 = 6$	**2** $x - 3 = 4$	**3** $6 - x = 3$	**4** $x + 5 = 9$
5 $x - 7 = 5$	**6** $13 - x = 6$	**7** $x + 2 = 7$	**8** $3 + x = 6$
9 $x - 5 = 7$	**10** $x - 5 = 2$	**11** $1 + x = 5$	**12** $8 + x = 13$
13 $x - 3 = 5$	**14** $x - 2 = 6$	**15** $x + 7 = 11$	**16** $x + 3 = 4$
17 $x - 2 = 5$	**18** $x + 4 = 7$	**19** $x - 8 = 4$	**20** $x + 9 = 15$
21 $4 - x = 1$	**22** $10 + x = 17$	**23** $10 - x = 1$	**24** $6 + x = 8$
25 $4 - x = 2$	**26** $4 + x = 4$	**27** $x + 10 = 13$	**28** $11 - x = 9$
29 $6 - x = 1$	**30** $12 + x = 15$		

39/ CONTINUING A NUMBER SEQUENCE

If you can spot the connection between the terms of a series, it is possible to say how the series will continue.

EXAMPLE

▶ State the next two terms in the sequence: 1, 4, 7, 10, ..., ...

The difference between consecutive terms is 3.
The next two terms are 13 and 16.

EXAMPLE

▶ State the next two terms in the sequence: 1, 3, 9, 27, ..., ...

Each term is multiplied by 3 to get the next.
The next two terms are $27 \times 3 = 81$ and $81 \times 3 = 243$.

Exercise 39A

State the next two terms in each sequence.

1 5, 7, 9, 11, ..., ...	**2** 23, 21, 19, 17, ..., ...	**3** 10, 20, 30, 40, ..., ...
4 7, 10, 13, 16, ..., ...	**5** 5, 10, 15, 20, ..., ...	**6** 11, 12, 13, 14, ..., ...
7 15, 18, 21, 24, ..., ...	**8** 1, 4, 9, 16, ..., ...	**9** 7, 13, 23, 37, ..., ...
10 4, 8, 12, 16, ..., ...	**11** 28, 26, 24, 22, ..., ...	**12** 12, 17, 22, 27, ..., ...
13 39, 37, 34, 30, ..., ...	**14** 26, 25, 24, 23, ..., ...	**15** –2, –4, –6, –8, ..., ...
16 47, 43, 39, 35, ..., ...	**17** 6, 12, 18, 24, ..., ...	**18** 55, 50, 45, 40, ..., ...
19 44, 51, 58, 65, ..., ...	**20** 14, 21, 28, 35, ..., ...	**21** $\frac{1}{4}$, $\frac{1}{2}$, 1, 2, ..., ...
22 1, 2, 4, 7, ..., ...	**23** 17, 16, 15, 14, ..., ...	**24** 80, 40, 20, 10, ..., ...
25 73, 69, 65, 61, ..., ...	**26** 2, 5, 10, 17, ..., ...	**27** 2, 4, 6, 8, ..., ...
28 7, 9, 11, 13, ..., ...	**29** 2, –1, –4, –7, ..., ...	**30** 47, 44, 40, 35, ..., ...

Exercise 39B

State the next two terms in each sequence.

1 12, 14, 16, 18, ..., ...	**2** 64, 61, 58, 55, ..., ...	**3** 10, 20, 30, 40, ..., ...
4 6, 7, 8, 9, ..., ...	**5** 98, 96, 94, 92, ..., ...	**6** 4, 8, 12, 16, ..., ...
7 9, 15, 21, 27, ..., ...	**8** 13, 17, 22, 28, ..., ...	**9** 2, 4, 8, 16, ..., ...
10 18, 21, 24, 27, ..., ...	**11** 24, 23, 22, 21, ..., ...	**12** 4, 7, 12, 19, ..., ...
13 1, 3, 5, 7, ..., ...	**14** 0, –1, –2, –3, ..., ...	**15** 256, 128, 64, 32, ..., ...
16 6, 11, 16, 21, ..., ...	**17** 78, 75, 71, 66, ..., ...	**18** 5, 10, 15, 20, ..., ...
19 8, 4, 2, 1, ..., ...	**20** 47, 43, 39, 35, ..., ...	**21** 1, 4, 9, 16, ..., ...
22 64, 56, 48, 40, ..., ...	**23** 7, $8\frac{1}{2}$, 10, $11\frac{1}{2}$, ..., ...	**24** 99, 90, 81, 72, ..., ...
25 10, 18, 26, 34, ..., ...	**26** 6, 9, 13, 18, ..., ...	**27** –5, –1, 3, 7, ..., ...
28 10, 20, 30, 40, ..., ...	**29** 61, 59, 57, 55, ..., ...	**30** 54, 50, 45, 39, ..., ...

40/ PREDICTING THE TERMS IN A SERIES

EXAMPLE

▶ The terms of a series are: 1st is 2, 2nd is 4, 3rd is 6, and 4th is 8.
State the connection between the terms and then state the 5th and 6th terms.

Each term in the series is 2 more than the previous term.
This means: 5th term = 10 and 6th term = 12.

EXAMPLE

▶ The terms of a series are: 1st is 3, 2nd is 6, 3rd is 9, and 4th is 12.
State the connection between the terms and then state the 7th and 10th terms.

Each term is a multiple of 3.
This means: 7th term = 21, and the 10th term = 30.

EXAMPLE

▶ The terms of a series are: 1st is 2, 2nd is 3, 3rd is 5, and 4th is 8.
State the connection between the terms and then state the 5th and 7th terms.

The difference between consecutive terms is increasing by 1.
This means: 5th term = 12 and the 7th term = 23. (Note: 6th term = 17)

Exercise 40A

You are given four terms of each series.
(a) State the connection between the terms of the series.
(b) State the missing terms indicated by a question mark.

Term	1st	2nd	3rd	4th	5th	6th	7th	8th	9th	10th
1	38	41	44	47	?	?				
2	9	10	11	12	?	?				
3	5	10	15	20	?		?			
4	14	17	20	23	?	?				
5	35	33	31	29	?			?		
6	6	12	18	24	?		?			
7	48	46	44	42		?		?		
8	20	25	30	35		?	?			
9	11	13	15	17		?		?		
10	3	6	9	12			?	?		
11	45	41	37	33			?	?		
12	10	17	24	31			?		?	
13	1	2	4	8			?	?		
14	4	8	12	16		?			?	
15	2		6	8	10			?		?
16	61	53	45	37	?		?			
17	7	8	9	10					?	?
18		48	43	38	33		?	?		
19	27	25		21	19				?	?
20	10	20	30	40					?	?

Exercise 40B

You are given four terms of each series.
(a) State the connection between the terms of the series.
(b) State the missing terms indicated with a question mark.

Term	1st	2nd	3rd	4th	5th	6th	7th	8th	9th	10th
1	12	16	20	24	?	?				
2	12	15	18	21	?	?				
3	8	17	32	53	?	?				
4	2	4	6	8	?			?		
5	19	25	31	37	?	?				
6	4	8	12	16		?			?	
7	35	37	39	41		?		?		
8	14	13	12	11		?				?
9	10	20	30	40		?			?	
10	20	21	22	23			?			?
11	11	13	15	17					?	?
12	46	42	37	31		?	?			
13	63	61	59	57				?		?
14	20	19	18	17					?	?
15	14	19	25	32	?	?				
16	2	4	8	16	?		?			
17	14		20	23	26		?		?	
18	20	28		44	52	?	?			
19	27	29	31			37		?		?
20	6	12	18	24			?			?

41/ COLLECTING LIKE TERMS

$a + a + a = 3a$

$4c + 3c = 7c$

$2ef + ef = 3ef$

$b + b = 2b$

$5d - 2d = 3d$

$7x - 6x = x$ (x is a better answer than $1x$)

BUT $2a + 3b$ does *not* equal $5a$ or $5b$ or $5ab$. You cannot simplify this any more, so $2a + 3b = 2a + 3b$.

EXAMPLE
▶ Simplify $2a + 7b - 3b + 4a$.

$2a + 4a + 7b - 3b = 6a + 4b$

EXAMPLE
▶ Show the meaning of $3a - 2b$.

$3a - 2b = a + a + a - b - b$

Exercise 41A

Simplify:

1 $a + a$

2 $b + b + b$

3 $d + d + d + d$

4 $e + e + e + e - e$

5 $b + 2b$

6 $c + 4c$

7 $3e - e$

8 $4a - 2a$

9 $5c - 4c$

10 $2d + 3d$

11 $a + 3a + 2a$

12 $2b + 4b + b$

| **13** $d + 4d + d$ | **14** $3e + 3e + 3e$ | **15** $6b - b + 3b - 4b$ | **16** $5a + 4b + 2b$ |
| **17** $3a + 4b$ | **18** $2a + 3b - 4c + 3a$ | **19** $2a - a + 6b - 5b$ | **20** $a + 4b + 3a + 2b$ |

Exercise 41B

Simplify:

1 $v + v + v$	**2** $w + w$	**3** $y + y$	**4** $z + z + z$
5 $2w + 2w$	**6** $4x - 3x$	**7** $5z + 4z$	**8** $6v - 2v$
9 $3x + 3x - 2x$	**10** $2y + 2y + 2y$	**11** $2v - 5v + 4v$	**12** $w + w + w + 3w$
13 $3y + 2y + y + 3y$	**14** $5z - 2z + z + 3z$	**15** $3w + 5v + 2v - 2w$	
16 $2x + 3x + x - 5y - 2x$	**17** $5x + 2x + y$	**18** $x + x + 3y - x - 5y + 2x$	
19 $7x + 3y - 3x + x$	**20** $6w - 5w + 7v - 6v$		

Exercise 41C

Show the meaning of the following using + and −.

1 $2a$	**2** $2b$	**3** $3d$	**4** $2e$
5 $5b$	**6** $2c$	**7** $5e$	**8** $2a + 2b$
9 $3c + 2d$	**10** $3d + e$	**11** $2a - 2b$	**12** $3b - c$
13 $2d + 3e$	**14** $2e - 3f$	**15** $3b + 2c$	**16** $2c - 3d$
17 $3e + 2f - g$	**18** $a + 2b + 2c$	**19** $c - 3d + 2e$	**20** $2d + 2e + 2f$

Exercise 41D

Show the meaning of the following using + and −.

1 $3v$	**2** $2w$	**3** $4y$	**4** $3z$
5 $4w$	**6** $3x$	**7** $6z$	**8** $2v + 2w$
9 $2x + 3y$	**10** $3y - z$	**11** $2w - 3v$	**12** $2w + 2x - z$
13 $5x - 3y$	**14** $2v - 2w$	**15** $w + 4x$	**16** $3x + y - z$
17 $2y - 3x - z$	**18** $3a - 2b + c$	**19** $3x - 3y$	**20** $2x - y - z$

42/ FUNCTION MACHINES: FINDING OUTPUTS

A **function machine** acts in the same way on each and every number that is put into the machine. These numbers are called the **input**. These numbers all leave the machine as **output**.

The function machine below multiplies each input number by 3 and then subtracts 2.

in $\rightarrow$ $\boxed{\times 3}$ $\rightarrow$ $\boxed{- 2}$ $\rightarrow$ out

Exercise 42A

State the *outputs* for the given inputs.

1　in → $\boxed{\times 2}$ → $\boxed{+1}$ → out

　　(a) 1　　(b) 3　　(c) 5　　(d) 7

2　in → $\boxed{\times 3}$ → $\boxed{-5}$ → out

　　(a) 10　(b) 8　　(c) 6　　(d) 4

3　in → $\boxed{\times 2}$ → $\boxed{+2}$ → out

　　(a) 1　　(b) 3　　(c) 5　　(d) 7

4　in → $\boxed{\div 2}$ → $\boxed{+1}$ → out

　　(a) 10　(b) 12　(c) 14　(d) 16

5　in → $\boxed{\times 7}$ → $\boxed{+1}$ → out

　　(a) 1　　(b) 2　　(c) 3　　(d) 4

6　in → $\boxed{\times 3}$ → $\boxed{-1}$ → out

　　(a) 10　(b) 11　(c) 12　(d) 13

7　in → $\boxed{\times 8}$ → $\boxed{+2}$ → out

　　(a) 2　　(b) 4　　(c) 6　　(d) 8

8　in → $\boxed{\times 6}$ → $\boxed{-5}$ → out

　　(a) 8　　(b) 6　　(c) 4　　(d) 2

9　in → $\boxed{\div 3}$ → $\boxed{+4}$ → out

　　(a) 3　　(b) 6　　(c) 9　　(d) 18

10　in → $\boxed{\times \frac{1}{4}}$ → $\boxed{+5}$ → out

　　(a) 24　(b) 20　(c) 16　(d) 12

Exercise 42B

State the *outputs* for the given inputs.

1　in → $\boxed{\times 4}$ → $\boxed{+1}$ → out

　　(a) 2　　(b) 4　　(c) 6　　(d) 8

2　in → $\boxed{\times 2}$ → $\boxed{-5}$ → out

　　(a) 3　　(b) 5　　(c) 7　　(d) 9

3　in → $\boxed{\div 2}$ → $\boxed{+1}$ → out

　　(a) 10　(b) 16　(c) 20　(d) 24

4　in → $\boxed{\times 3}$ → $\boxed{-10}$ → out

　　(a) 50　(b) 40　(c) 20　(d) 10

5　in → $\boxed{\times 9}$ → $\boxed{-5}$ → out

　　(a) 1　　(b) 3　　(c) 5　　(d) 25

6　in → $\boxed{\times 2}$ → $\boxed{+5}$ → out

　　(a) 10　(b) 12　(c) 14　(d) 40

7　in → $\boxed{\div 5}$ → $\boxed{+2}$ → out

　　(a) 0　　(b) 5　　(c) 10　(d) 100

8　in → $\boxed{\times 3}$ → $\boxed{+2}$ → out

　　(a) 2　　(b) 4　　(c) 6　　(d) 50

9　in → $\boxed{\times 4}$ → $\boxed{+3}$ → out

　　(a) 2　　(b) 4　　(c) 8　　(d) 32

10　in → $\boxed{\times \frac{1}{2}}$ → $\boxed{-8}$ → out

　　(a) 64　(b) 32　(c) 16　(d) 2

43/ FUNCTION MACHINES: FINDING INPUTS

If the output is given and the question is to find the input, you must remember to reverse the function *completely*. This means reversing the order as well.

For example, if the function is $\boxed{\times 2} \to \boxed{+ 5}$ then the reverse is '– 5' followed by '÷ 2'.

EXAMPLE

▶ in $\to \boxed{\times 2} \to \boxed{+ 1} \to$ out

State the input for each output given:
      (a) 7   (b) 9   (c) 11   (d) 31

This means that the function needs to be reversed: '– 1' then '÷ 2'.
Inputs:
    (a) $7 \to \boxed{- 1} \to 6 \to \boxed{÷ 2} \to 3$
    (b) $9 \to \boxed{- 1} \to 8 \to \boxed{÷ 2} \to 4$
    (c) $11 \to \boxed{- 1} \to 10 \to \boxed{÷ 2} \to 5$
    (d) $31 \to \boxed{- 1} \to 30 \to \boxed{÷ 2} \to 15$

Exercise 43A

State the *inputs* for the given outputs.

1 in $\to \boxed{\times 3} \to \boxed{- 2} \to$ out
    (a) 7 (b) 10 (c) 13 (d) 16

2 in $\to \boxed{÷ 2} \to \boxed{+ 1} \to$ out
    (a) 7 (b) 6 (c) 5 (d) 4

3 in $\to \boxed{\times 2} \to \boxed{- 4} \to$ out
    (a) 8 (b) 6 (c) 4 (d) 2

4 in $\to \boxed{÷ 3} \to \boxed{+ 1} \to$ out
    (a) 1 (b) 2 (c) 3 (d) 4

5 in $\to \boxed{\times 5} \to \boxed{+ 2} \to$ out
    (a) 17 (b) 22 (c) 27 (d) 32

6 in $\to \boxed{÷ 3} \to \boxed{- 4} \to$ out
    (a) 3 (b) 4 (c) 5 (d) 20

7 in $\to \boxed{\times 2} \to \boxed{+ 1} \to$ out
    (a) 9 (b) 11 (c) 13 (d) 51

8 in $\to \boxed{÷ 4} \to \boxed{+ 3} \to$ out
    (a) 3 (b) 4 (c) 5 (d) 6

9 in $\to \boxed{\times 5} \to \boxed{- 3} \to$ out
    (a) 22 (b) 27 (c) 32 (d) 52

10 in $\to \boxed{\times \frac{1}{2}} \to \boxed{- 1} \to$ out
    (a) 0 (b) 1 (c) 2 (d) 15

Exercise 43B

State the *inputs* for the given outputs.

1 in $\to \boxed{÷ 2} \to \boxed{+ 3} \to$ out
    (a) 5 (b) 6 (c) 7 (d) 8

2 in $\to \boxed{\times 2} \to \boxed{+ 1} \to$ out
    (a) 11 (b) 13 (c) 15 (d) 17

3 in $\to \boxed{÷ 3} \to \boxed{- 5} \to$ out
    (a) 6 (b) 7 (c) 8 (d) 9

4 in $\to \boxed{\times 3} \to \boxed{- 8} \to$ out
    (a) 40 (b) 37 (c) 34 (d) 31

5 in $\to \boxed{÷ 5} \to \boxed{+ 2} \to$ out
    (a) 2 (b) 3 (c) 4 (d) 20

6 in $\to \boxed{\times 5} \to \boxed{+ 4} \to$ out
    (a) 14 (b) 24 (c) 34 (d) 104

7 in $\rightarrow$ $\boxed{\div 2}$ $\rightarrow$ $\boxed{-6}$ $\rightarrow$ out

    (a) 0   (b) 2   (c) 4   (d) 100

9 in $\rightarrow$ $\boxed{\times 3}$ $\rightarrow$ $\boxed{+1}$ $\rightarrow$ out

    (a) 7   (b) 13   (c) 19   (d) 37

8 in $\rightarrow$ $\boxed{\div 6}$ $\rightarrow$ $\boxed{-2}$ $\rightarrow$ out

    (a) 4   (b) 3   (c) 2   (d) 98

10 in $\rightarrow$ $\boxed{\times \frac{1}{4}}$ $\rightarrow$ $\boxed{-3}$ $\rightarrow$ out

    (a) 0   (b) 1   (c) 2   (d) 7

44/ FUNCTION MACHINES: FINDING INPUTS AND OUTPUTS

Previous exercises have dealt with inputs and outputs for function machines. The exercises below have mixed questions. In some questions you need to find the output given the input and in other questions you need to find the input given the output.

EXAMPLE

▶ 2, 3, 4, 5 $\rightarrow$ $\boxed{\times 3}$ $\rightarrow$ $\boxed{-2}$ $\rightarrow$?

    Outputs: 4, 7, 10, 13

EXAMPLE

▶ ? $\rightarrow$ $\boxed{\times 2}$ $\rightarrow$ $\boxed{-3}$ $\rightarrow$ 21, 27, 33, 39

    Inputs: 12, 15, 18, 21

Exercise 44A

State the missing inputs or outputs:

1 2, 3, 4, 5 $\boxed{\times 2}$ $\rightarrow$ $\boxed{-1}$ $\rightarrow$?

3 ? $\rightarrow$ $\boxed{\times 2}$ $\rightarrow$ $\boxed{+1}$ $\rightarrow$ 11, 13, 15, 17

5 0, 1, 2, 3 $\rightarrow$ $\boxed{\times 2}$ $\rightarrow$ $\boxed{+2}$ $\rightarrow$?

7 ? $\rightarrow$ $\boxed{\times 2}$ $\rightarrow$ $\boxed{-3}$ $\rightarrow$ 1, 3, 5, 7

9 5, 6, 7, 8 $\rightarrow$ $\boxed{\times 2}$ $\rightarrow$ $\boxed{+3}$ $\rightarrow$?

11 ? $\rightarrow$ $\boxed{\times 3}$ $\rightarrow$ $\boxed{+3}$ $\rightarrow$ 12, 15, 18, 21

13 1, 2, 3, 4 $\rightarrow$ $\boxed{\times 6}$ $\rightarrow$ $\boxed{-1}$ $\rightarrow$?

15 ? $\rightarrow$ $\boxed{\div 2}$ $\rightarrow$ $\boxed{-1}$ $\rightarrow$ 1, 3, 5, 7

17 2, 3, 4, 5 $\rightarrow$ $\boxed{\times 5}$ $\rightarrow$ $\boxed{-1}$ $\rightarrow$?

19 2, 3, 4, 5 $\rightarrow$ $\boxed{\times 7}$ $\rightarrow$ $\boxed{+2}$ $\rightarrow$?

2 1, 2, 3, 4 $\rightarrow$ $\boxed{\times 3}$ $\rightarrow$ $\boxed{-2}$ $\rightarrow$?

4 ? $\rightarrow$ $\boxed{\div 2}$ $\rightarrow$ $\boxed{-1}$ $\rightarrow$ 5, 6, 7, 8

6 0, 2, 4, 6 $\rightarrow$ $\boxed{\div 2}$ $\rightarrow$ $\boxed{+1}$ $\rightarrow$?

8 ? $\rightarrow$ $\boxed{\div 3}$ $\rightarrow$ $\boxed{-3}$ $\rightarrow$ 2, 3, 4, 5

10 2, 4, 6, 8 $\rightarrow$ $\boxed{\div 2}$ $\rightarrow$ $\boxed{-1}$ $\rightarrow$?

12 ? $\rightarrow$ $\boxed{\div 2}$ $\rightarrow$ $\boxed{-2}$ $\rightarrow$ 2, 4, 6, 8

14 9, 15, 21, 27 $\rightarrow$ $\boxed{\div 3}$ $\rightarrow$ $\boxed{+2}$ $\rightarrow$?

16 ? $\rightarrow$ $\boxed{\times 2}$ $\rightarrow$ $\boxed{+5}$ $\rightarrow$ 17, 19, 21, 23

18 ? $\rightarrow$ $\boxed{\times 3}$ $\rightarrow$ $\boxed{+2}$ $\rightarrow$ 8, 11, 14, 17

20 ? $\rightarrow$ $\boxed{\div 5}$ $\rightarrow$ $\boxed{-4}$ $\rightarrow$ 1, 2, 3, 4

Exercise 44B

State the missing inputs or outputs.

1 1, 2, 3, 4 $\rightarrow$ $\boxed{\times 2}$ $\rightarrow$ $\boxed{-1}$ $\rightarrow$?

3 3, 6, 9, 12 $\rightarrow$ $\boxed{\div 3}$ $\rightarrow$ $\boxed{+1}$ $\rightarrow$?

5 ? $\rightarrow$ $\boxed{\times 2}$ $\rightarrow$ $\boxed{+2}$ $\rightarrow$ 4, 6, 8, 10

7 1, 2, 3, 4 $\rightarrow$ $\boxed{\times 3}$ $\rightarrow$ $\boxed{-3}$ $\rightarrow$?

9 ? $\rightarrow$ $\boxed{\div 4}$ $\rightarrow$ $\boxed{+3}$ $\rightarrow$ 5, 6, 7, 8

2 2, 3, 4, 5 $\rightarrow$ $\boxed{\times 3}$ $\rightarrow$ $\boxed{-2}$ $\rightarrow$?

4 ? $\rightarrow$ $\boxed{\div 2}$ $\rightarrow$ $\boxed{-3}$ $\rightarrow$ 3, 5, 7, 9

6 ? $\rightarrow$ $\boxed{\times 4}$ $\rightarrow$ $\boxed{-2}$ $\rightarrow$ 10, 14, 18, 22

8 5, 6, 7, 8 $\rightarrow$ $\boxed{\times 4}$ $\rightarrow$ $\boxed{+2}$ $\rightarrow$?

10 ? $\rightarrow$ $\boxed{\times 5}$ $\rightarrow$ $\boxed{-7}$ $\rightarrow$ 3, 8, 13, 18

11 6, 8, 10, 12 → $\boxed{\div 2}$ → $\boxed{-2}$ → ?

12 1, 2, 3, 4 → $\boxed{\times 5}$ → $\boxed{+3}$ → ?

13 ? → $\boxed{\div 3}$ → $\boxed{-2}$ → 1, 2, 3, 4

14 ? → $\boxed{\times 2}$ → $\boxed{+1}$ → 1, 3, 5, 7

15 1, 2, 3, 4 → $\boxed{\times 2}$ → $\boxed{-3}$ → ?

16 3, 5, 7, 9 → $\boxed{\times 2}$ → $\boxed{+1}$ → ?

17 ? → $\boxed{\times 3}$ → $\boxed{-1}$ → 11, 14, 17, 20

18 2, 3, 4, 5 → $\boxed{\times 4}$ → $\boxed{-1}$ → ?

19 ? → $\boxed{\div 3}$ → $\boxed{-5}$ → 1, 2, 3, 4

20 1, 2, 3, 4 → $\boxed{\times 5}$ → $\boxed{-3}$ → ?

45/ FUNCTION MACHINES: FINDING THE FUNCTION

In these two exercises the inputs and outputs are given; you are required to find out what function is needed in the function machine.

EXAMPLE

▶ Find the missing function:

10, 11, 12, 13 → $\boxed{?}$ → 15, 16, 17, 18

The function is '+ 5'.

EXAMPLE

▶ Find the missing function:

0, 1, 2, 3 → $\boxed{?}$ → 5, 7, 9, 11

You can see that the inputs increase by only 1 but the output increases by 2. This tells you that the function contains '× 2'. You then need to decide how much you need to add or subtract.

The function is '× 2' and then '+ 5'.

Exercise 45A

Find the missing functions.

1 10, 11, 12, 13→ $\boxed{?}$ → 12, 13, 14, 15

2 6, 8, 10, 12 → $\boxed{?}$ → 5, 7, 9, 11

3 2, 4, 6, 8 → $\boxed{?}$ → 4, 8, 12, 16

4 5, 6, 7, 8 → $\boxed{?}$ → 0, 1, 2, 3

5 1, 3, 5, 7 → $\boxed{?}$ → 5, 7, 9, 11

6 1, 2, 3, 4 → $\boxed{?}$ → 2, 4, 6, 8

7 9, 8, 7, 6 → $\boxed{?}$ → 19, 18, 17, 16

8 5, 9, 13, 17 → $\boxed{?}$ → 1, 5, 9, 13

9 2, 3, 4, 5 → $\boxed{?}$ → 14, 21, 28, 35

10 24, 20, 16, 12 → $\boxed{?}$ → 12, 10, 8, 6

11 9, 8, 7, 6 → $\boxed{?}$ → 6, 5, 4, 3

12 3, 5, 7, 9 → $\boxed{?}$ → 9, 15, 21, 27

13 10, 12, 14, 16 → $\boxed{?}$ → 8, 10, 12, 14

14 8, 12, 16, 20 → $\boxed{?}$ → 2, 3, 4, 5

15 4, 3, 2, 1 → $\boxed{?}$ → 24, 18, 12, 6

16 50, 40, 30, 20 → $\boxed{?}$ → 10, 8, 6, 4

17 21, 24, 27, 30 → $\boxed{?}$ → 7, 8, 9, 10

18 5, 4, 3, 2 → $\boxed{?}$ → 50, 40, 30, 20

19 18, 15, 12, 9 → $\boxed{?}$ → 10, 7, 4, 1

20 2, 3, 4, 5 → $\boxed{?}$ → 10, 15, 20, 25

Exercise 45B

Find the missing functions.

1 7, 9, 11, 13 → ? → 3, 5, 7, 9

2 9, 8, 7, 6 → ? → 12, 11, 10, 9

3 8, 6, 4, 2 → ? → 4, 3, 2, 1

4 8, 6, 4, 2 → ? → 12, 10, 8, 6

5 0, 3, 6, 9 → ? → 0, 6, 12, 18

6 30, 40, 50, 60 → ? → 3, 4, 5, 6

7 2, 4, 6, 8 → ? → 4, 6, 8, 10

8 3, 4, 5, 6 → ? → 15, 20, 25, 30

9 1, 2, 3, 4 → ? → 2, 3, 4, 5

10 6, 5, 4, 3 → ? → 3, 2, 1, 0

11 20, 22, 24, 26 → ? → 10, 12, 14, 16

12 6, 12, 18, 24 → ? → 1, 2, 3, 4

13 0, 2, 4, 6 → ? → 0, 6, 12, 18

14 0, 4, 8, 12 → ? → 5, 9, 13, 17

15 32, 28, 24, 20 → ? → 8, 7, 6, 5

16 0, 2, 4, 6 → ? → 0, 14, 28, 42

17 7, 5, 3, 1 → ? → 14, 10, 6, 2

18 2, 4, 6, 8 → ? → 1, 2, 3, 4

19 25, 30, 35, 40 → ? → 5, 6, 7, 8

20 1, 2, 3, 4 → ? → 10, 20, 30, 40

Exercise 45C

State the function required.

1 2, 4, 6, 8 → ? → 1, 2, 3, 4

2 1, 3, 5, 7 → ? → 4, 8, 12, 16

3 3, 2, 1, 0 → ? → 8, 7, 6, 5

4 8, 9, 10, 11 → ? → 1, 2, 3, 4

5 2, 6, 10, 14 → ? → 3, 7, 11, 15

6 1, 3, 5, 7 → ? → 3, 9, 15, 21

7 1, 2, 3, 4 → ? → 5, 10, 15, 20

8 8, 6, 4, 2 → ? → 17, 13, 9, 5

9 6, 4, 2, 0 → ? → 14, 10, 6, 2

10 2, 4, 6, 8 → ? → 2, 3, 4, 5

11 10, 8, 6, 4 → ? → 5, 4, 3, 2

12 2, 4, 6, 8 → ? → 5, 9, 13, 17

13 14, 10, 6, 2 → ? → 7, 5, 3, 1

14 1, 3, 5, 7 → ? → 3, 7, 11, 15

15 0, 1, 2, 3 → ? → 3, 5, 7, 9

16 1, 2, 3, 4 → ? → 3, 4, 5, 6

17 10, 11, 12, 13 → ? → 1, 2, 3, 4

18 11, 9, 7, 5 → ? → 7, 6, 5, 4

19 1, 3, 5, 7 → ? → 1, 5, 9, 13

20 0, 1, 2, 3 → ? → 3, 5, 7, 9

Exercise 45D

State the function required.

1 1, 2, 3, 4 → ? → 2, 4, 6, 8

2 2, 4, 6, 8 → ? → 1, 2, 3, 4

3 2, 3, 4, 5 → ? → 6, 9, 12, 15

4 4, 3, 2, 1 → ? → 8, 6, 4, 2

5 3, 6, 9, 12 → ? → 1, 2, 3, 4

6 1, 2, 3, 4 → ? → 5, 10, 15, 20

7 7, 5, 3, 1 → ? → 11, 9, 7, 5

8 12, 9, 6, 3 → ? → 4, 3, 2, 1

9 2, 4, 6, 8 → ? → 2, 6, 10, 14

10 0, 5, 10, 15 → ? → 0, 1, 2, 3

11 0, 1, 2, 3 → ? → 0, 6, 12, 18

12 1, 3, 5, 7 → ? → 1, 5, 9, 13

13 14, 10, 6, 2 → ? → 12, 8, 4, 0

14 6, 4, 2, 0 → ? → 13, 9, 5, 1

15 15, 10, 5, 0 → ⬜ ? → 3, 2, 1, 0

16 7, 5, 3, 1 → ⬜ ? → 12, 10, 8, 6

17 0, 1, 2, 3 → ⬜ ? → 2, 4, 6, 8

18 4, 3, 2, 1 → ⬜ ? → 3, 2, 1, 0

19 5, 4, 3, 2 → ⬜ ? → 11, 9, 7, 5

20 6, 7, 8, 9 → ⬜ ? → 12, 14, 16, 18

REVISION

Exercise C

1 Find the value that is missing from ⬜ that makes each equation true.
   (a) ⬜ × 5 = 20
   (b) 4 + ⬜ = 10
   (c) 11 − ⬜ = 2
   (d) 36 ÷ ⬜ = 9
   (e) ⬜ × 6 = 30
   (f) 45 ÷ ⬜ = 5
   (g) ⬜ − 3 = 10
   (h) 5 + ⬜ = 12

2 Solve these equations.
   (a) $x - 7 = 5$
   (b) $7 + x = 11$
   (c) $12 - x = 9$
   (d) $x + 2 = 8$
   (e) $12 + x = 20$
   (f) $7 - x = 5$
   (g) $\frac{x}{2} = 3$
   (h) $2x = 12$

3 State the next two terms in each sequence.
   (a) 5, 7, 9, 11, ... , ...   (b) 56, 45, 34, 23, ... , ...   (c) 2, 3, 5, 8, ... , ...   (d) 3, 6, 9, 12, ... , ...

4 State the next two terms in each sequence and state the connection between the terms.
   (a) 5, 10, 15, 20, ... , ...   (b) 1, 2, 4, 7, ... , ...   (c) 80, 78, 75, 71, ... , ...   (d) 1, 2, 4, 8, ... , ...

5 Simplify:
   (a) $g + g$
   (b) $2h + 3h$
   (c) $5i - 4i$
   (d) $2j + 3k - k + 3j$

6 Show the meaning of the following using + and − .
   (a) $3p$
   (b) $5q$
   (c) $3r - 2s$
   (d) $2t + 2u - w$

7 in → ×3 → +1 → out
   State the *outputs* for these inputs: (a) 2   (b) 4   (c) 6   (d) 10

8 in → ×2 → −1 → out
   State the *outputs* for these inputs: (a) 1   (b) 3   (c) 5   (d) 7

9 in → ×2 → −1 → out
   State the *inputs* for these outputs: (a) 5   (b) 7   (c) 9   (d) 13

10 in → ÷2 → +3 → out
   State the *inputs* for these outputs: (a) 6   (b) 7   (c) 8   (d) 10

11 Find the missing functions.
   (a) 1, 2, 3, 4 → ⬜ ? → 5, 6, 7, 8
   (b) 2, 4, 6, 8 → ⬜ ? → 4, 8, 12, 16
   (c) 1, 3 ,5, 7 → ⬜ ? → 0, 2, 4, 6
   (d) 2, 4, 6, 8 → ⬜ ? → 6, 12, 18, 24

Exercise CC

1 You are given four terms of each series.
(i) State the connection between the terms of the series.
(ii) State the terms indicated.

(a)
1st term	21
2nd term	23
3rd term	25
4th term	27

State the 5th and 7th terms.

(b)
1st term	35
2nd term	32
3rd term	29
4th term	26

State the 6th and 7th terms.

(c)
1st term	1
2nd term	2
3rd term	4
4th term	8

State the 5th and 6th terms.

(d)
2nd term	15
3rd term	25
4th term	35
5th term	45

State the 1st and 7th terms.

2 Each table shows the terms in a series. Copy and complete the tables and fill in the missing quantities:

(a)
Term number	1	2	3	4	5	6	7	8
Term	10	12		16		20		

(b)
Term number	1	2	3	4	6	8	10	12
Term		5	7	10		32		

3 State the missing inputs or outputs.
(a)   2, 4, 6, 8 → $÷2$ → -1 → ?
(b)   ? → $×2$ → -1 → 13, 15, 17, 21
(c)   1, 2, 3, 4 → $×5$ → $+2$ → ?
(d)   ? → $÷3$ → $+1$ → 2, 4, 6, 10

4 Simon finds a pattern of numbers: 100, 91, 82, 73, ...
He continues the pattern but stops when he finds that the next term will be less than 0. What is the last term that Simon writes and how many terms are there in the pattern altogether (including the original terms and Simon's)?

5 Jaspal is drawing in the back of her book to pass the time until the end of the lesson.
She draws the pattern shown in the diagram.
She continues the pattern by drawing more rows *underneath* the bottom row.
Copy and complete the table below.

+ +
+ + +
+ + + +

Row number	Number of + in row	Total of + in pattern so far
1	2	2
2	3	5
3		
4		
6		
10		

What is the difference between the total for the pattern with 100 rows and the total for the pattern with 99 rows?

2a means $2 \times a$

a^2 means $a \times a$

ab means $a \times b$

2ab means $2 \times a \times b$

$3a^2$ means $3 \times a \times a$

$a \div b$ can be written as $\dfrac{a}{b}$

$a \div 2$ can be written as $\dfrac{a}{2}$ or $\dfrac{1}{2}a$

$2a \div 3b$ can be written as $\dfrac{2a}{3b}$

$2a \div 4b$ can be written as $\dfrac{2a}{4b}$ and then cancelled to $\dfrac{a}{2b}$

EXAMPLE

▶ Show the meaning of (a) $3bc$ (b) $\dfrac{2a}{b}$

(a) $3bc = 3 \times b \times c$

(b) $\dfrac{2a}{b} = 2 \times a \div b$

EXAMPLE

▶ Simplify (a) $a \times b$ (b) $2a \times 3a$ (c) $a \div 2c$ (d) $3a \div 6a$ (e) $a^2 \div a$

(a) $a \times b = ab$

(b) $2a \times 3a = 6a^2$

(d) $3a \div 6a = \dfrac{3a}{6a}$

$\quad = \dfrac{a}{2a}$ (cancel by 3)

$\quad = \dfrac{1}{2}$ (cancel by a)

(c) $a \div 2c = \dfrac{a}{2c}$

(e) $a^2 \div a = \dfrac{a^2}{a}$

$\quad = a$ (cancel by a)

Exercise 46A

Show the meaning of the following.

1 ab	**2** bc	**3** $3d$	**4** $2de$	**5** $5bc$
6 b^2	**7** $3a^2$	**8** $\dfrac{a}{b}$	**9** $\dfrac{c}{d}$	**10** $\dfrac{2a}{b}$
11 $\dfrac{a^2}{b}$	**12** $\dfrac{5c}{3}$	**13** $\dfrac{c^2}{d}$	**14** $\dfrac{4a}{c}$	**15** $\dfrac{d}{e}$
16 e^2	**17** $\dfrac{a^2}{a}$	**18** $\dfrac{5b}{2}$	**19** abc	**20** $2abc$

Exercise 46B

Show the meaning of the following.

1 pq	**2** qr	**3** $5t$	**4** $3pq$	**5** p^2
6 q^2	**7** $3r^2$	**8** $\dfrac{p}{q}$	**9** $\dfrac{2r}{s}$	**10** $\dfrac{3q}{5}$
11 $\dfrac{r^2}{p}$	**12** $\dfrac{2r}{3}$	**13** $\dfrac{s^2}{3}$	**14** $3q$	**15** $\dfrac{t^2}{2}$

16 $2t^2$	**17** $2pqr$	**18** $\dfrac{p^2}{q}$	**19** stu	**20** s^2t

Exercise 46C

Simplify:

1 $a \div b$	**2** $a \times b$	**3** $a \times a$	**4** $b \times c$
5 $a \div 2$	**6** $2 \div a$	**7** $d \div 5$	**8** $5 \times d$
9 $2 \times a \times b$	**10** $3 \times e \times e$	**11** $7 \times b \div c$	**12** $a \times b \div 2$
13 $6 \div b$	**14** $c \div 7$	**15** $a \times b \div c$	**16** $3 \times d \times e \div 5$
17 $2 \times b \times 3 \times c$	**18** $3 \times b \times c \times d$	**19** $3 \times c \div 4$	**20** $b \times b \times c$

Exercise 46D

Simplify:

1 $p \times r$	**2** $q \times s$	**3** $2 \times p$	**4** $2 \times p \times p$
5 $3 \div q$	**6** $r \div 4$	**7** $t \div u$	**8** $s \times t$
9 $3 \times s \times t$	**10** $5 \times s \times s$	**11** $p \times q \div 3$	**12** $s \times s \div t$
13 $q \times r \div 2$	**14** $s^2 \div p$	**15** $p \times q \times r \div 4$	**16** $1 \div p$
17 $2 \times p \times p$	**18** $2 \times p \times p \times q$	**19** $10 \times s \div t$	**20** $3 \times s \times t \times u$

47/ MULTIPLYING OUT BRACKETS

$2(x + 1)$ means 'two lots of $(x + 1)$'.
$2(x + 1) = 2x + 2$

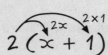

> **EXAMPLE**
>
> ▶ Multiply out: (a) $3(a - 2)$ (b) $3(2c + 4)$.
>
> (a) $3(a - 2) = 3 \times a - 3 \times 2$ (b) $3(2c + 4) = 3 \times 2c + 3 \times 4$
> $\qquad\qquad\quad = 3a - 6$ $\qquad\qquad\qquad\qquad = 6c + 12$

Exercise 47A

Multiply out the brackets.

1 $2(a + 3)$	**2** $3(x - 4)$	**3** $4(5 - b)$	**4** $2(c + 6)$
5 $5(x + 2)$	**6** $3(2 - a)$	**7** $2(x + 4)$	**8** $5(a - 3)$
9 $3(6 + b)$	**10** $2(a + b)$	**11** $3(x - y)$	**12** $5(a + b)$
13 $2(x + y)$	**14** $4(a - b)$	**15** $3(a + b)$	**16** $7(x - y)$
17 $2(a - b)$	**18** $4(x + y)$	**19** $5(x - 3)$	**20** $3(a + 4)$
21 $2(3 + 2a)$	**22** $3(2a - 3)$	**23** $5(2x - 1)$	**24** $2(2a + 3)$
25 $4(1 - 3b)$	**26** $2(5 + 2c)$	**27** $2(2a - b)$	**28** $3(2x + 5y)$
29 $5(4b - 2)$	**30** $3(2a - 3b)$		

Exercise 47B

Multiply out the brackets.

1	$2(s-3)$	**2**	$5(p+2)$	**3**	$3(4-q)$	**4**	$5(5-p)$
5	$2(r+3)$	**6**	$4(s+1)$	**7**	$2(s+6)$	**8**	$3(p-4)$
9	$2(3+q)$	**10**	$2(s-t)$	**11**	$3(p+q)$	**12**	$4(p+q)$
13	$5(s+t)$	**14**	$3(p+q)$	**15**	$2(p-q)$	**16**	$7(s-t)$
17	$6(p-q)$	**18**	$3(s+t)$	**19**	$4(s-3)$	**20**	$3(p+3)$
21	$3(2+3p)$	**22**	$2(2p-1)$	**23**	$5(2s-3)$	**24**	$3(3p+4)$
25	$5(1-2q)$	**26**	$2(5+2r)$	**27**	$3(2p-3q)$	**28**	$4(3s+5t)$
29	$2(5q-8)$	**30**	$3(3p-4q)$				

48/ SUBSTITUTION INTO ALGEBRAIC EXPRESSIONS

Remember: ab means $a \times b$

$2a$ means $2 \times a$

$2abc$ means $2 \times a \times b \times c$

$\dfrac{a}{b}$ means $a \div b$

a^2 means $a \times a$

$\dfrac{(a+b)}{2}$ means 'add a and b, then divide the total by 2'

In these exercises the value of each letter will be given. The purpose of each question is to find the value of the expression if the values are substituted into that expression.

EXAMPLE

▶ Use $a = 2$, $b = 3$, $c = 4$ and $d = 5$ to find the value of:

(a) $2b$ (b) d^2 (c) $a + b$ (d) $2(c + d)$ (e) $\dfrac{6a}{c}$

(a) $2b = 2 \times b$ (b) $d^2 = d \times d$ (c) $a + b = 2 + 3$

       $= 2 \times 3$ $= 5 \times 5$ $= 5$

       $= 6$ $= 25$

(d) $2(c + d) = 2 \times (4 + 5)$ (e) $\dfrac{6a}{c} = \dfrac{12}{3}$

             $= 2 \times 9$ $= 12 \div 3$

             $= 18$ $= 4$

Exercise 48A

Use $a = 5$, $b = 2$ and $c = 4$, to calculate the value of the following.

1	$2a$	**2**	$5c$	**3**	$3b$	**4**	$a + b$	**5**	$a - c$
6	ab	**7**	bc	**8**	ac	**9**	$\dfrac{c}{b}$	**10**	$\dfrac{10}{a}$
11	$\dfrac{6b}{c}$	**12**	$2ab$	**13**	$3ac$	**14**	$5bc$	**15**	a^2

Use $a = 4$, $b = 1$ and $c = 3$, to calculate the value of the following.

16	b^2	17	c^2	18	$2a^2$	19	$(2a)^2$	20	$2a + 3c$
21	$3b - c$	22	$3c + a$	23	$5a - 2c$	24	$7c + 2a$	25	$4b + 5c$
26	$2(a + b)$	27	$2(c - b)$	28	$3(a + c)$	29	$5(a - c)$	30	$4(b + c)$

Exercise 48B

Use $p = 8$, $q = 4$, $r = 1$ and $s = 2$ to calculate the value of the following.

1	$3r$	2	$2p$	3	$4q$	4	$p + q$	5	$p - q$
6	pq	7	qr	8	rs	9	$\dfrac{q}{r}$	10	$\dfrac{12}{p}$
11	$\dfrac{6q}{p}$	12	$5rs$	13	$2pr$	14	$3qr$	15	p^2

Use $p = 3$, $q = 10$, $r = 2$ and $s = 1$ to calculate the value of the following.

16	q^2	17	s^2	18	$(2p)^2$	19	$2p^2$	20	$3p + 2q$
21	$q - 3r$	22	$5p + 2r$	23	$6r + 2p$	24	$3q - 5p$	25	$2r + 3s$
26	$2(p + q)$	27	$3(q - p)$	28	$2(r + s)$	29	$4(q - 2p)$	30	$5(p + r)$

49/ EQUATIONS AND FORMULAE IN WORDS

EXAMPLE

▶ I think of a number and subtract 5. When I double my answer I get 12. What was my original number?

I must have doubled 6 to get 12.
This means that my original number must have been 11.

EXAMPLE

▶ The perimeter of a rectangle is found by adding the width and height and then multiplying the answer by 2. What is the perimeter of a rectangle which has a width of 5 cm and a height of 7 cm?

Height + width = 5 + 7
= 12 cm
Perimeter = 2 × 12
= 24 cm
(Do not forget to put the units for the answer: cm in this case.)

Exercise 49A

1 I think of a number and multiply it by 5. This gives me forty-five. What is the number?

2 Ishfaq cuts 15 cm from a length of wood. If this leaves him with 35 cm, how long was the piece of wood?

3 I think of a number and then take away 8. If the answer is 4, what is the number?

4 The perimeter of a square is found by multiplying the length of a side by four. If the perimeter of a square is 24 cm, what is the length of a side?

5 The temperature has fallen by 5°C to 9°C. What was the starting temperature?

6 Yogesh has used 95 minutes of his tape. He has 85 minutes left. How many minutes does the tape last?

7 One-quarter of a number is seven. What is the number?

8 John is twice as old as Rachel. If John is fourteen, how old is Rachel?

9 I think of a number and add 5. The result is 12. What was the number?

10 A triangle has three equal angles. The total of the angles in a triangle is 180°. What is the size of each angle?

11 I think of a number and add 4. The result is 10. What was the number?

12 The area of a rectangle is found by multiplying the width by the height. If the area is 36 cm^2 and the width is 9 cm, what is the height?

13 I think of a number and double it. This gives me 18. What was the number?

14 The distance travelled in a given time is found by multiplying the speed by the time. How far does a car travel in 4 hours at a steady speed of 67 miles per hour?

15 Paul's tape lasts for 240 minutes. If he has recorded two programmes of equal length and has 160 minutes remaining, how long did each programme last?

16 I think of a number and then take away 9. If the answer is 4, what is the number?

17 The time taken to travel a given distance is found by dividing the distance travelled by the speed. Find the time taken to travel 225 km at 75 km per hour.

18 Gillian has twelve packets of *Bombay Mixture* but has only two left after a party. How many packets were used?

19 I think of a number and then take away 3. If the answer is 7, what is the number?

20 I think of a number and double it. This gives me 20. What is the number?

21 Georgia is half the age of David. If Georgia is ten years old, how old is David?

22 I think of a number and multiply it by three. This gives me 21. What is the number?

23 The cost of hiring a chain-saw is £9 plus a charge for each day it is hired. If the total cost for two days is £31, what is the charge per day?

24 Laurie cuts 32 cm from a length of wood. If this leaves him with 68 cm, how long was the piece of wood?

25 Double an angle is 84°. What is the angle?

26 I think of a number and add 3. The result is 11. What was the number?

27 In a recipe the amount of stock used is twice the amount of water. If Don uses 120 ml of stock, how much water should he use?

28 One-third of a number is 5. What is the number?

29 The temperature rises by 5°C to 18°C. What was the starting temperature?

30 Taj and Sue share £18 so that Taj has half as much as Sue. How much did Sue have?

Exercise 49B

1 One-quarter of a number is 4. What is the number?

2 In one year from now Sid will be eight and Karen will be twice as old. How old is Karen now?

3 I think of a number, double it and subtract 7 to get 19. What was the number?

4 The area of a parallelogram is found by multiplying the base by the height. If the area is 18 cm² and the base is 6 cm, what is the height?

5 I think of a number and subtract 7 before dividing by 2 to get 5. What is the number?

6 In two years time Betty will be six and Barry will be twice as old. How old is Barry now?

7 Bob goes out jogging on three mornings. He jogs equal distances on the first and third days. He jogs 8 km on the second day. If the total distance that Bob jogs is 20 km, how far does he jog on the first day?

8 I think of a number and then take away 3. If the answer is 8, what is the number?

9 Colin and Elaine share £100 so that Colin has £50 more than Elaine. How much does Colin receive?

10 The sum of the angles in a triangle is 180°. Fiona measures one angle and finds that it is 50°. She knows that the other two angles are equal to each other. What is the size of each of the equal angles?

11 A number is multiplied by 6 to give 36. What is the number?

12 The cost of hiring a car is £33 plus £51 per day. For how many days does Norman hire the car if the total cost is £186?

13 Four is added to half a number to give eleven. What is the number?

14 Josh weighs twice as much as Stephanie. Their total weight is 87 kg. How much does Josh weigh?

15 Some 25p stamps and a 20p stamp cost £1.70. How many 25p stamps are there?

16 I add 3 to a number and then multiply by 4 to give 48. What is the number?

17 Nigel buys a box of eggs. He breaks half of them and then uses four. He has five unbroken eggs remaining. How many eggs were in the box when he bought it?

18 I think of a number and add 6. The result is 13. What was the number?

19 I double a number and add 8. This gives me 16. What was the number?

20 Half a number is eight. What is the number?

21 The perimeter of a rectangle is found by adding the width to the height and then multiplying this total by 2. What is the perimeter of rectangle if the width is 6 cm and the height is 7 cm?

22 Mo calculates the circumference of a circle by multiplying the diameter by 3. What is the diameter of a circle that he calculates to have a circumference of 27 cm?

23 I add 1 to a number and then halve the result to get 9. What was the number?

24 Donna gives away half of her sweets and then eats three. This leaves her with seven sweets. How many did she have originally?

25 A box of tiles contains four more blue tiles than white tiles. The total number of tiles in the box is 36. How many white tiles are there?

26 Ben needs to buy eighteen presents. He goes shopping on three days. He buys the same number on the first and second days and then buys four on the third day. How many presents did he buy on the second day?

27 I think of a number and add 3 to it. I then multiply the total by 3 to give 27. What is the number?

28 A number is doubled and then 5 is added. This gives 17. What is the number?

29 A firm makes clocks and then packs them in boxes of six. The box and packing materials weigh 1200 grams. The total weight of the box containing the six clocks is 6000 grams. How much does each clock weigh?

30 Four packets of crisps and a 50-gram packet of nuts weigh 170 grams. What is the weight of one packet of crisps?

50/ WRITING ALGEBRAIC EQUATIONS

Sometimes an actual number answer is not needed. There are times when the answer shows how to obtain a value later when more information is available.

EXAMPLE

▶ How many days are there in *n* weeks?

There are 7 days in 1 week.
There are 2 × 7 days in 2 weeks.
There are *n* × 7 or 7*n* days in *n* weeks.

EXAMPLE

▶ What length remains after *b* cm has been cut from 90 cm?

The length *b* cm must be subtracted from the original 90 cm.
Remaining length = 90 − *b* cm

EXAMPLE

▶ Diedre earns £*a* but already has £*b*. How much does she have altogether?

Add to find the total.
She has £*a* + £*b* which can be written £(*a* + *b*).

Exercise 50A

Write an expression for each of the following.

1 *b* more than 7

2 6 less than *c*

3 3 times *d*

4 *f* divided by 5

5 5 more than *e*

6 *e* less than 8

7 1 divided by *b*

8 *g* times *h*

9 *g* more than *h*

10 *p* times *q*

11 10 divided by *c*

12 3 less than *b*

13 12 more than *d*

14 the product of *x* and *y*

15 *d* divided by 3

Write the answers to the following questions as algebraic expressions.

16 What is the total length of 10 pieces of wood that are each *d* cm long?

17 I know that my total journey time is *h* hours. How much time remains after *n* hours?

18 There are *g* girls in a class and *b* boys. How many pupils are there in the class?

19 Samira earns £3 per hour. How much does she earn in *h* hours?

20 The total area of the circle in the diagram is *A* cm². What is the area of the shaded section?

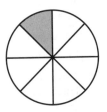

21 What is the total width of *c* cans if each can has a width of 6 cm?

22 What is the total area of floor covering required if the hall needs *h* square metres and the porch needs *p* square metres?

23 There are 52 people on a coach trip. Of these, *n* get off at the first stop. How many are left?

24 How many days are there in *w* weeks?

25 What is the total of *b* and twice *c*?

26 Richie earns £*a* in one week and £*b* the following week. How much does he earn over the two weeks?

27 Tom writes a series of numbers: 1, 3, 5, 7, ... When he gets to the number *n*, what is the next number in the series?

28 A cake is cut into *n* pieces. What fraction of the cake is each piece?

29 Nancy has *x* pence and Gillian has twice as much. How much do they have in total?

30 What is the number of the question which follows the *m*th question?

Exercise 50B

Write an expression for each of the following.

1 *c* more than 20	**2** 10 less than *a*	**3** 8 divided by *a*
4 9 times *f*	**5** *r* divided by *s*	**6** *p* more than *q*
7 *g* less than *h*	**8** the total of *r* and *s*	**9** *c* times 7
10 *e* divided by 4	**11** the product of *s* and *t*	**12** 6 more than *f*
13 6 times *e*	**14** the difference between *s* and *t*	**15** *t* divided by *u*

Write the answers to the following questions as algebraic expressions.

16 Tim travels for *m* minutes on a bus and *n* minutes on a train. What is the total time taken for the journey?

17 How much time is left on a 180-minute tape if *m* minutes have been used?

18 How many metres are there in *k* kilometres?

19 Ahmed earns £*P* in 32 hours. How much does he earn per hour?

20 Herman has saved £*S* but has to spend £*n*. How much does he have left?

21 The curved section of the shape in the diagram measures *a* cm and the straight section is *b* cm.

What is the perimeter (total distance around the outside) of the shape?

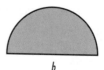

22 What is the total weight of ten coins each weighing *c* grams?

23 It takes Polly 54 seconds to run one lap. How long does it take her to run *q* laps at this speed?

24 The weight of a computer is *k* kg but the weight of its packing is *p* kg. What is the total weight of the computer and packing?

25 The total area of the shape in the diagram is *A* cm². The shaded area is *B* cm².

What is the area of the unshaded part?

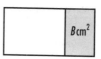

26 What is the total weight of *n* nails weighing *x* grams each?

27 How many minutes are there in *y* seconds?

28 What is twice the total of *a* and *b*?

29 Jason has £*J*. He spends three-quarters of it. What sum of money remains?

30 What is the question number before the *n*th question?

51/ SUBSTITUTING INTO SIMPLE FORMULAE

EXAMPLE

▶ The area of a triangle is given by the formula: $A = \frac{1}{2}bh$

Find the area if (a) $b = 7$ cm and $h = 8$ cm (b) $b = 12$ cm and $h = 9$ cm.

(a) $A = \frac{1}{2} \times 7 \times 8$
$= 28$ cm^2

(b) $A = \frac{1}{2} \times 12 \times 9$
$= 54$ cm^2

EXAMPLE

▶ The area of a trapezium is given by the formula:
$A = \frac{1}{2}(a + b)h$
Find the value of A when $a = 3$ cm, $b = 7$ cm, and $h = 5$ cm.

$A = \frac{1}{2}(a + b)h$
$= \frac{1}{2} \times (3 + 7) \times 5$
$= \frac{1}{2} \times 10 \times 5$
$= 25$ cm^2

Exercise 51A

1 $W = mg$
Find the value of W when (a) $m = 6$ and $g = 10$ (b) $m = 8$ and $g = 9.8$.

2 $A = lw$
Find the value of A when (a) $l = 4$ and $w = 5$ (b) $l = 3.2$ and $w = 10$.

3 $P = 2(b + h)$
Find the value of P when (a) $b = 6$ and $h = 4$ (b) $b = 4.5$ and $h = 4$.

4 $v = \dfrac{s}{t}$
Find the value of v when (a) $s = 120$ and $t = 2$ (b) $s = 160$ and $t = 5$.

5 $x = \dfrac{1}{2}(a + b)$
Find the value of x when (a) $a = 8$ and $b = 10$ (b) $a = 3$ and $b = 4$.

6 $A = l^2$
Find the value of A when (a) $l = 5$ (b) $l = 1.5$.

7 $s = \dfrac{p}{100}$
Find the value of s when (a) $p = 500$ (b) $p = 454$.

8 $A = \dfrac{1}{2}h(a + b)$
Find the value of A when (a) $a = 2$, $b = 4$ and $h = 6$ (b) $a = 3$, $b = 5$ and $h = 5$.

9 $h = \dfrac{m}{60}$
Find the value of h when (a) $m = 180$ (b) $m = 270$.

10 $I = \dfrac{V}{R}$
Find the value of I when (a) $V = 300$ and $R = 60$ (b) $V = 240$ and $R = 1200$.

11 $M = mv$

Find the value of M when   (a) $m = 12$ and $v = 3$ (b) $m = 5$ and $v = 2.4$.

12 $A = 3r^2$

Find the value of A when   (a) $r = 4$ (b) $r = 10$.

13 $P = mgh$

Find the value of P when   (a) $m = 5$, $g = 10$ and $h = 9$ (b) $m = 4$, $g = 9.8$ and $h = 20$.

14 $R = \dfrac{100I}{PT}$

Find the value of R when   (a) $I = 50$, $P = 200$ and $T = 5$ (b) $I = 42$, $P = 250$ and $T = 4$.

15 $A = 2\pi rh$

Find the value of A when   (a) $\pi = 3$, $r = 4$ and $h = 5$ (b) $\pi = 3.1$, $r = 2$ and $h = 5$.

16 $V = a^2 h$

Find the value of V when   (a) $a = 4$ and $h = 5$ (b) $a = 10$ and $h = 2.5$.

17 $F = \dfrac{x\lambda}{a}$

Find the value of F when   (a) $\lambda = 6$, $x = 3$ and $a = 2$ (b) $\lambda = 4$, $x = 2.5$ and $a = 5$.

18 $V = lwh$

Find the value of V when   (a) $l = 3$, $w = 4$ and $h = 5$ (b) $l = 7.5$, $w = 2$ and $h = 10$.

19 $C = \dfrac{5(F - 32)}{9}$

Find the value of C when   (a) $F = 68$ (b) $F = 95$.

20 $r = \dfrac{C}{2\pi}$

Find the value of r when   (a) $C = 72$ and $\pi = 3$ (b) $C = 62$ and $\pi = 3.1$.

Exercise 51B

1 $m = 60h$

Find the value of m when   (a) $h = 4$ (b) $h = 2.5$.

2 $V = IR$

Find the value of V when   (a) $I = 2$ and $R = 32$ (b) $I = 0.001$ and $R = 500$.

3 $p = 100s$

Find the value of p when   (a) $s = 5$ (b) $s = 3.6$.

4 $C = 3d$

Find the value of C when   (a) $d = 10$ (b) $d = 6.2$.

5 $T = 2n - 4$

Find the value of T when   (a) $n = 8$ (b) $n = 20$.

6 $v = u + at$

Find the value of v when   (a) $u = 5$, $a = 10$ and $t = 2$ (b) $u = 4$, $a = 9.8$ and $t = 5$.

7 $A = \dfrac{1}{2}bh$

Find the value of A when   (a) $b = 14$ and $h = 8$ (b) $b = 76$ and $h = 50$.

8 $s = vt$

Find the value of s when   (a) $v = 40$ and $t = 2$ (b) $v = 65$ and $t = 4$.

9 $L = 4(a + b + c)$

Find the value of L when   (a) $a = 1$, $b = 2$ and $c = 2$ (b) $a = 2$, $b = 3$ and $c = 5$.

10 $m = \dfrac{a + b + c}{3}$

Find the value of m when   (a) $a = 4$, $b = 5$ and $c = 6$ (b) $a = 5$, $b = 7$ and $c = 9$.

11 $t = \dfrac{d}{s}$

Find the value of t when (a) $d = 240$ and $s = 60$ (b) $d = 100$ and $s = 2.5$.

12 $F = 1.8C + 32$

Find the value of F when (a) $C = 10$ (b) $C = 20$

13 $y = mx + c$

Find the value of y when (a) $m = 2$, $x = 5$ and $c = 3$ (b) $m = \dfrac{1}{2}$, $x = 4$ and $c = 3$.

14 $K = \dfrac{1}{2} mv^2$

Find the value of K when (a) $m = 50$ and $v = 3$ (b) $m = 5$ and $v = 4$.

15 $I = \dfrac{PRT}{100}$

Find the value of I when (a) $P = 100$, $R = 10$ and $T = 2$ (b) $P = 500$, $R = 18$ and $T = 4$.

16 $c = a^2 + b^2$

Find the value of c when (a) $a = 4$ and $b = 3$ (b) $a = 4$ and $b = 2$.

17 $d = 5t^2$

Find the value of d when (a) $t = 4$ (b) $t = 0.2$.

18 $R = \dfrac{V}{I}$

Find the value of R when (a) $V = 120$ and $I = 4$ (b) $V = 240$ and $I = 10$.

19 $P = I^2R$

Find the value of P when (a) $I = 1$ and $R = 10$ (b) $I = 5$ and $R = 20$.

20 $A = a^2 + 4ab$

Find the value of A when (a) $a = 6$ and $b = 0$ (b) $a = 6$ and $b = 1$.

52/ NAMING POINTS IN THE FIRST QUADRANT

Remember: When finding the coordinates of a point find the x value (along) first and the y value (up) second.

EXAMPLE

▶ State the coordinates of the points in the diagram.

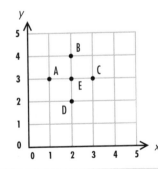

$A = (1, 3)$ $B = (2, 4)$ $C = (3, 3)$
$D = (2, 2)$ $E = (2, 3)$

Exercise 52A

For each diagram, state the coordinates of the labelled points.

1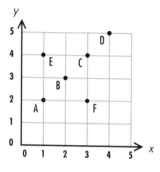

2

3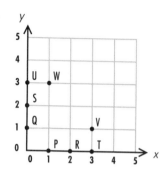

4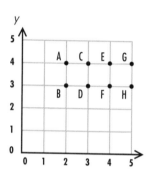

5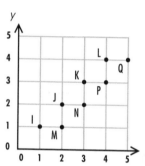

6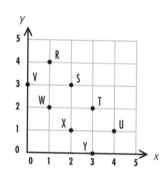

Exercise 52B

For each diagram, state the coordinates of the labelled points.

1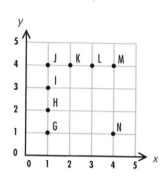

2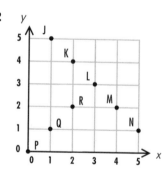

3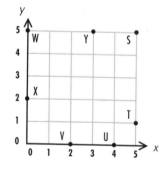

4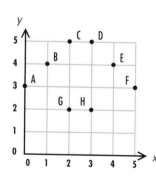

5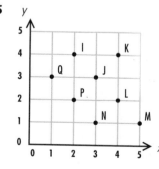

6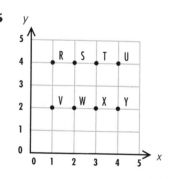

For each question you will need to draw axes on a 5 × 5 grid (use squared paper).

EXAMPLE

► Plot and label the points:
A = (2, 3)
B = (2, 4)
C = (3, 5)
D = (4, 5)

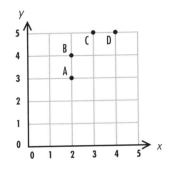

Exercise 53A

For each of the questions, draw axes on a 5 × 5 grid, then plot and label the points.

1 A = (1, 1), B = (2, 2), C = (3, 3) and D = (4, 4)

2 E = (5, 0), F = (4, 1), G = (3, 2) and H = (2, 3)

3 I = (1, 1), J = (1, 2), K = (1, 3) and L = (1, 4)

4 M = (2, 2), N = (3, 2), P = (4, 2) and Q = (5, 2)

5 R = (1, 2), S = (1, 4), T = (3, 2) and U = (3, 4)

6 V = (5, 2), W = (5, 5), X = (3, 1) and Y = (3, 2)

7 A = (2, 1), B = (3, 2), C = (4, 3) and D = (5, 4)

8 E = (0, 0), F = (0, 5), G = (5, 0) and H = (5, 5)

9 I = (2, 3), J = (3, 4), K = (4, 5) and L = (5, 4)

10 M = (0, 4), N = (1, 3), P = (2, 2) and Q = (3, 1)

Exercise 53B

For each of the questions, draw axes on a 5 × 5 grid, then plot and label the points.

1 A = (4, 1), B = (3, 2), C = (2, 1) and D = (1, 0)

2 E = (2, 0), F = (3, 1), G = (4, 2) and H = (5, 3)

3 I = (2, 5), J = (3, 5), K = (2, 0) and L = (4, 0)

4 M = (5, 3), N = (5, 1), P = (0, 4) and Q = (0, 2)

5 R = (4, 3), S = (3, 5), T = (2, 1) and U = (1, 5)

6 V = (4, 1), W = (3, 1), X = (2, 2) and Y = (3, 2)

7 A = (5, 0), B = (5, 1), C = (5, 3) and D = (5, 5)

8 E = (0, 0), F = (1, 1), G = (1, 2) and H = (2, 4)

9 I = (3, 4), J = (2, 3), K = (1, 5) and L = (2, 4)

10 M = (0, 4), N = (4, 0), P = (1, 4) and Q = (4, 1)

Exercise 53C

For each question draw axes on a 5 × 5 grid.
Plot the points and join them together as instructed to draw various shapes.

1 Join (1, 1) to (2, 1) to (3, 1).
Join (3, 1) to (3, 2) to (3, 3) to (3, 4) to (3, 5).
Join (1, 3) to (2, 3) to (3, 3).
Join (1, 5) to (2, 5) to (3, 5).

2 Join (3, 3) to (4, 3) to (5, 3).
Join (1, 5) to (2, 5) to (3, 5) to (4, 5).
Join (4, 1) to (4, 2) to (4, 3) to (4, 4)
    to (4, 5).

3 Join (1, 1) to (2, 1) to (3, 1).
Join (2, 1) to (2, 2) to (2, 3) to (2, 4).
Join (1, 3) to (2, 4).

4 Join (1, 1) to (2, 1) to (3, 1).
Join (1, 3) to (2, 3) to (3, 3).
Join (1, 5) to (2, 5) to (3, 5).
Join (1, 5) to (1, 4) to (1, 3) to (1, 2) to (1, 1).
Join (3, 5) to (3, 4) to (3, 3) to (3, 2) to (3, 1).

5 Join (1, 5) to (1, 4) to (1, 3) to (1, 2).
Join (3, 5) to (3, 4) to (3, 3) to (3, 2) to
    (3, 1) to (3, 0).
Join (1, 2) to (2, 2) to (3, 2) to (4, 2) to (5, 2).

6 Join (1, 4) to (2, 4) to (3, 4).
Join (1, 1) to (2, 1) to (3, 1).
Join (1, 2) to (2, 2) to (3, 2).
Join (3, 4) to (3, 3) to (3, 2).
Join (1, 2) to (1, 1).

7 Join (3, 5) to (4, 5) to (5, 5).
Join (3, 5) to (3, 4) to (3, 3) to (3, 2) to (3, 1).
Join (3, 3) to (4, 3) to (5, 3).
Join (3, 1) to (4, 1) to (5, 1).

8 Join (2, 1) to (3, 1) to (4, 1).
Join (2, 3) to (3, 3) to (4, 3).
Join (2, 5) to (3, 5) to (4, 5).
Join (4, 3) to (4, 2) to (4, 1).
Join (2, 3) to (2, 4) to (2, 5).

Exercise 53D

For each question draw axes on a 5 × 5 grid.
Plot the points and join them together as instructed to draw various shapes.

1 Join (3, 1) to (3, 2) to (3, 3) to (3, 4) to (3, 5).
Join (1, 5) to (2, 5) to (3, 5) to (4, 5) to (5, 5).

2 Join (1, 1) to (2, 3) to (3, 5).
Join (5, 1) to (4, 3) to (3, 5).
Join (2, 3) to (3, 3) to (4, 3).

3 Join (2, 1) to (2, 2) to (2, 3) to (2, 4) to (2, 5).
Join (2, 3) to (3, 3) to (4, 3).
Join (2, 5) to (3, 5) to (4, 5).

4 Join (1, 1) to (1, 2) to (1, 3) to (1, 4) to (1, 5).
Join (3, 1) to (2, 2) to (1, 3).
Join (3, 5) to (2, 4) to (1, 3).

5 Join (3, 0) to (3, 1) to (3, 2) to (3, 3).
Join (5, 0) to (5, 1) to (5, 2) to (5, 3).
Join (3, $1\frac{1}{2}$) to (4, $1\frac{1}{2}$) to (5, $1\frac{1}{2}$).

6 Join (3, 1) to (4, 1) to (5, 1).
Join (3, 4) to (3, 3) to (3, 2) to (3, 1).
Join (5, 4) to (4, 4) to (3, 4).
Join (3, $2\frac{1}{2}$) to (4, $2\frac{1}{2}$) to (5, $2\frac{1}{2}$).

7 Join (3, 1) to (3, 2) to (3, 3) to (3, 4).
Join (1, 4) to (1, 3) to (1, 2) to (1, 1).
Join (3, 1) to (2, $2\frac{1}{2}$) to (1, 4).

8 Join (1, 5) to (2, 5) to (3, 5).
Join (1, 5) to (1, 4) to (1, 3) to (1, 2).
Join (3, 2) to (2, 2) to (1, 2).
Join ($2\frac{1}{2}$, 3) to ($3\frac{1}{2}$, 3).
Join (3, 2) to (3, 3).

It is known that: 1 inch   = 2.54 cm
Therefore: 2 inches = 5.08 cm
                  3 inches = 7.62 cm etc.

This information can be plotted on a graph of centimetres against inches.

In practice plotting lots of points for a straight line is a bit of a waste of time; two points are normally enough but it is wise to plot a third point as a check that the line is straight.

In the graph shown 0 inches = 0 cm is plotted as (0, 0) and 10 inches = 25.4 cm is plotted as (10, 25.4). These two points are joined by a straight line. This line contains all the points of conversion between 0 inches and 10 inches. This is a **conversion graph**.

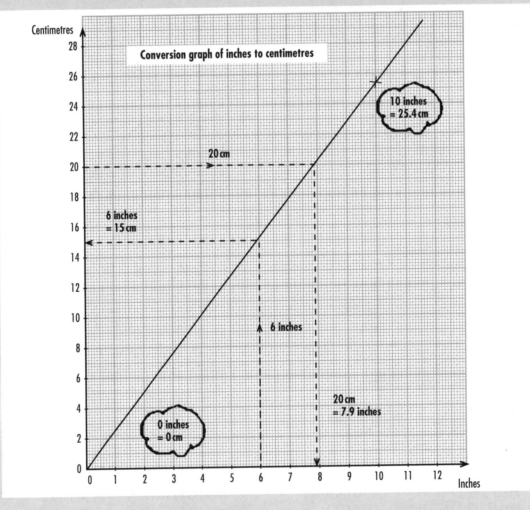

The conversion graph can be used to convert inches to centimetres and also to convert centimetres to inches.

For example you can read off that 20 cm is approximately 7.9 inches.

Also, 6 inches is approximately 15 cm.

Exercise 54A

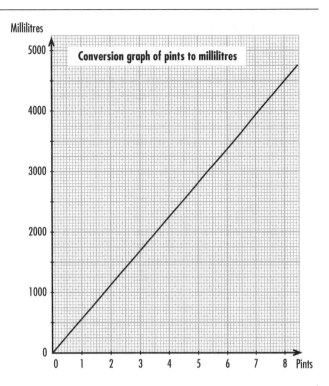

1 The graph converts pints to millilitres.

(a) Use the graph to convert the following to millilitres (to the nearest 50 ml):
2 pints, 5 pints, $6\frac{1}{2}$ pints, 5.7 pints

(b) Use the graph to convert the following to pints (to the nearest 0.1 pint):
3500 ml, 2250 ml, 1700 ml, 5100 ml

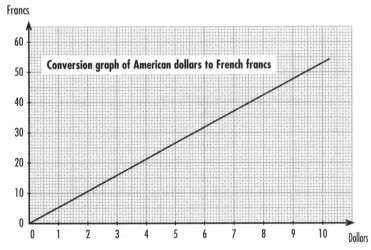

2 The graph converts US dollars to French francs.

(a) Use the graph to convert the following to francs:
$4, $8.50, $2.90, $5.40

(b) Use the graph to convert the following to dollars (to the nearest $0.10):
36 francs, 27 francs, 42 francs, 19 francs

3 On graph paper draw a 10-cm horizontal axis using 1 cm to represent 1 in² (square inch).
Draw a 6-cm vertical axis using 1 cm to represent 10 cm².
Plot the point that represents 9 in² = 58 cm².
(a) Use your graph to convert the following to square centimetres: 5 in², 7 in², 2.5 in², 7.5 in²
(b) Use your graph to convert the following to square inches: 40 cm², 27 cm², 20 cm², 25 cm²

4 On graph paper draw a 8-cm horizontal axis using 1 cm to represent 10 fl. oz (fluid ounces).
Draw a 12-cm vertical axis using 1 cm to represent 200 ml.
Plot the point that represents 35 fl. oz = 1000 ml.
(a) Use your graph to convert the following to millilitres: 63 fl. oz, 28 fl. oz, 7 fl. oz, 56 fl. oz
(b) Use your graph to convert the following to fluid ounces: 1400 ml, 2000 ml, 1200 ml, 400 ml

5 On graph paper draw a 8-cm horizontal axis using 1 cm to represent £1.
Draw a 15-cm vertical axis using 1 cm to represent $NZ 1 (New Zealand dollar).
Plot the point that represents £6 = $NZ 14.70.
 (a) Use your graph to convert the following to dollars: £2, £6.20, £3.80, £5.50
 (b) Use your graph to convert the following to pounds: $NZ 10.00, $NZ 12.50, $NZ 7.60, $NZ 12.00

6 On graph paper draw a 10-cm horizontal axis using 1 cm to represent 100 litres.
Draw a 12-cm vertical axis using 1 cm to represent 20 gallons.
Plot the point that represents 1000 litres = 220 gallons.
 (a) Use your graph to convert the following to gallons: 900 *l*, 180 *l*, 450 *l*, 360 *l*
 (b) Use your graph to convert the following to litres: 150 gal, 90 gal, 50 gal, 40 gal

7 On graph paper draw a 12-cm horizontal axis using 1 cm to represent 1000 metres.
Draw a 12-cm vertical axis using 1 cm to represent 1000 yards.
Plot the point that represents 10 000 m = 10 900 yd.
 (a) Use your graph to convert the following to yards: 4200 m, 7000 m, 11 000 m, 7800 m
 (b) Use your graph to convert the following to metres: 10 000 yd, 6000 yd, 2400 yd, 9600 yd

8 On graph paper draw a 10-cm horizontal axis using 1 cm to represent £5.
Draw a 12-cm vertical axis using 1 cm to represent 10 000 lire.
Plot the point that represents £40 = 100 000 lire.
 (a) Use your graph to convert the following to lire: £3.60, £30, £5, £24
 (b) Use your graph to convert the following to pounds: 90 000 lire, 12 000 lire, 20 000 lire, 30 000 lire

Exercise 54B

1 The graph converts degrees Celsius (°C) to degrees Fahrenheit (°F).

 (a) Use the graph to convert the following to degrees Fahrenheit:
 85°C, 30°C, 10°C, 38°C

 (b) Use the graph to convert the following to degrees Celsius:
 95°F, 75°F, 140°F, 52°F

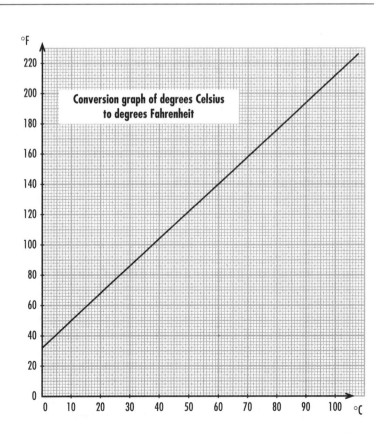

Conversion graph of degrees Celsius to degrees Fahrenheit

2 The graph converts pounds to Australian dollars ($A).

(a) Use the graph to convert the following to dollars:
£760, £500, £380, £600

(b) Use the graph to convert the following to pounds:
$A 400, $A 840, $A 1680, $A 1950

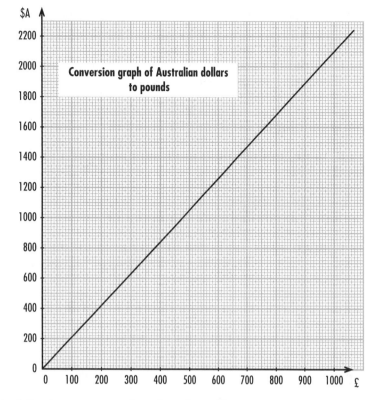

Conversion graph of Australian dollars to pounds

3 On graph paper draw a 8-cm horizontal axis using 1 cm to represent 2 ounces (oz).
Draw a 10-cm vertical axis using 1 cm to represent 50 gram.
Plot the point that represents 15 oz = 425 g.

(a) Use your graph to convert the following to grams: 6 oz, 5 oz, 9 oz, 12 oz

(b) Use your graph to convert the following to ounces: 80 g, 215 g, 305 g, 85 g

4 On graph paper draw a 10-cm horizontal axis using 1 cm to represent 10 square centimetres (cm^2).
Draw a 8-cm vertical axis using 1 cm to represent 2 square inches (in^2).
Plot the point that represents 100 cm^2 = 15.5 in^2.

(a) Use your graph to convert the following to in^2: 44 cm^2, 36 cm^2, 22 cm^2, 84 cm^2

(b) Use your graph to convert the following to cm^2: 11.0 in^2, 2.0 in^2, 9.0 in^2, 4.0 in^2

5 On graph paper draw a 10-cm horizontal axis using 1 cm to represent $10.
Draw a 13-cm vertical axis using 1 cm to represent 1000 pta (pesetas).
Plot the point that represents $100 = 13 000 pta.

(a) Use your graph to convert the following to pesetas: $70, $40, $14, $84

(b) Use your graph to convert the following to dollars: 7800 pta, 6500 pta, 4400 pta, 7000 pta

6 On graph paper draw a 10-cm horizontal axis using 1 cm to represent 200 kg.
Draw a 10-cm vertical axis using 1 cm to represent 500 lb (pound weight).
Plot the point that represents 2000 kg = 4400 lb.

(a) Use your graph to convert the following to pounds: 1500 kg, 940 kg, 1200 kg, 1800 kg

(b) Use your graph to convert the following to kilograms: 3600 lb, 2250 lb, 1100 lb, 1650 lb

7 On graph paper draw a 10-cm horizontal axis using 1 cm to represent 1 litre (*l*).
Draw a 10-cm vertical axis using 1 cm to represent 2 pints.
Plot the point that represents 10 *l* = 17.6 pints.

(a) Use your graph to convert the following to pints: 8 *l*, 5.8 *l*, 4 *l*, 6.6 *l*

(b) Use your graph to convert the following to litres: 18 pints, 12 pints, 19 pints, 6 pints

8 On graph paper draw a 10-cm horizontal axis using 1 cm to represent 1 mile.
Draw a 10-cm vertical axis using 1 cm to represent 2 km.
Plot the point that represents 10 miles = 16 km.
(a) Use your graph to convert the following to kilometres: 7.5 miles, 3.8 miles, 8.8 miles, 5 miles
(b) Use your graph to convert the following to miles: 4 km, 6.4 km, 5 km, 10 km

REVISION

Exercise $\triangleright$

1 Show the meaning of the following:
(a) fg (b) h^2 (c) $3fg$ (d) $\dfrac{h}{5}$ (e) $4f^2$ (f) $(3e)^2$ (g) $\dfrac{3f}{5}$ (h) $\dfrac{s}{t}$

2 Multiply out the brackets:
(a) $2(x + 4)$ (b) $5(x - 3)$ (c) $3(y + 1)$ (d) $5(4 - y)$

3 Use $p = 4$, $q = 3$, $r = 1$ and $s = 0$ to calculate the value of the following:
(a) $3p$ (b) $4q - 3p$ (c) $2p + 3r$ (d) ps

4 Use $v = 3$, $w = 5$, $x = 8$ and $y = 1$ to calculate the value of the following:
(a) vw (b) w^2 (c) $6(x + y)$ (d) $(w - y)^2$

5 Write the number that is:
(a) 5 more than w (b) 3 times p (c) p divided by q (d) r less than 10

6 Use the formula $x = p^2 - 5pq$ to find the value of x when:
(a) $p = 5$ and $q = 1$ (b) $p = 10$ and $q = 2$

7 State the coordinates of the points in the diagram.

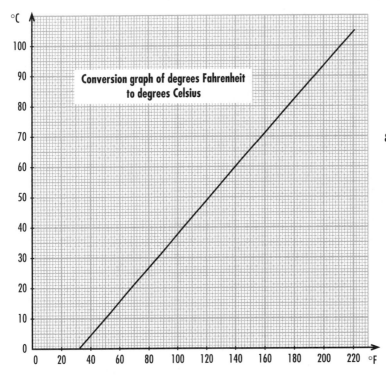

8 The graph converts degrees Fahrenheit (°F) to degrees Celsius (°C).

(a) Use the graph to convert the following to °C:
48°F, 176°F, 68°F, 200°F

(b) Use the graph to convert the following to °F:
5°C, 25°C, 50°C, 15°C

Exercise DD

1. Tim thinks of a number adds 2 and multiplies by 3 to get an answer of 21. What was the number?

2. Rob has some sweets. Charles eats half of them and then Gemma eats five. Rob still has ten left. How many did he have at the start?

3. The three angles in a triangle add up to 180°. If one angle of a triangle is 39° and another is 111°, what is the size of the third angle?

4. Harry cuts five equal pieces from a 60-cm length of wood. He still has 30 cm left. How long was each piece?

5. This year Meena is twice as old as her brother. Next year her brother will be seven. How old is Meena this year?

6. Jean cuts a piece of material in half and then cuts off a further 5 cm. She finds that the piece remaining measures 37 cm. How long was the piece of material originally?

7. Two numbers multiplied together give an answer of 32. One number is twice the size of the other. What is the larger number?

8. A number plus twice that number is 36. What is the number?

9. How many days are there in w weeks?

10. The cost of three chairs is £C. What is the cost of one chair?

11. Paula has m mice. She buys two more. How many does she have now?

12. The area of a rectangle is given by the formula $A = a(a + 3)$.
    (a) What is the area when $a = 4$ cm?
    (b) What is the value of a if $A = 70$ square centimetres?

13. Copy the 5 × 5 axes in the diagram. Plot the following points and join them up as indicated to draw a shape.

    Join (0, 5) to (2, 4) to (4, 3).
    Join (0, 1) to (2, 2) to (4, 3).
    Join (2, 4) to (2, 3) to (2, 2).

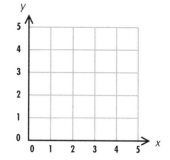

14. Given that £1 = 155 Japanese yen, draw a conversion graph for pounds to yen. Use 2 cm to represent £20 on the horizontal axis up to £100 and use 1 cm to represent 1000 yen on the vertical axis up to 16 000 yen.
    Copy the table below and use your graph to fill in the missing values.

Pounds	20			58	26		60	
Yen		6200	10 000			7000		15 000

Shape, space and measures

55/ ANGLES

Exercise 55A

Measure each of the following angles.

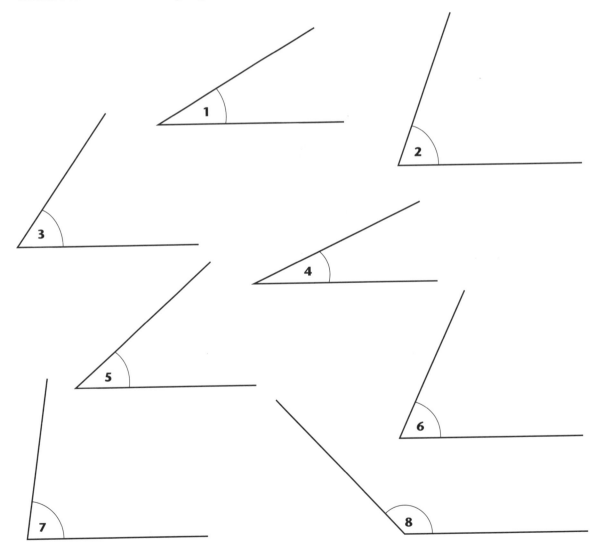

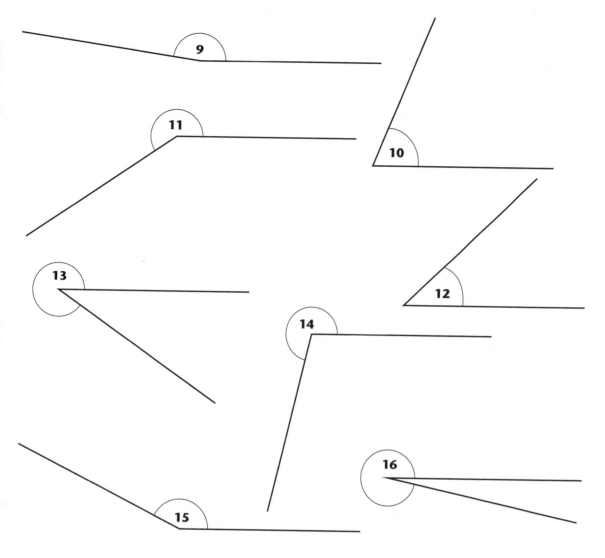

Exercise 55B

Measure each of the following angles.

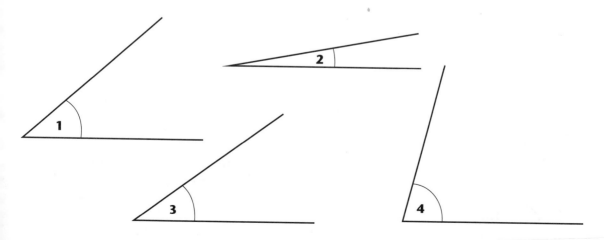

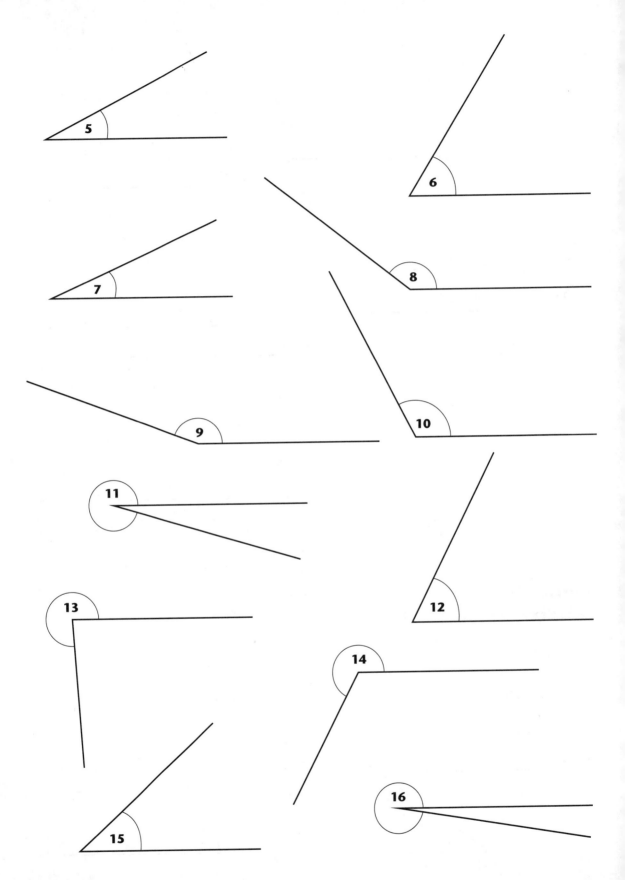

Exercise 55C

Draw each of the following angles.

1 20°	**2** 60°	**3** 15°	**4** 85°	**5** 63°
6 21°	**7** 34°	**8** 47°	**9** 72°	**10** 105°
11 176°	**12** 129°	**13** 32°	**14** 102°	**15** 228°
16 319°	**17** 84°	**18** 259°	**19** 115°	**20** 305°
21 271°	**22** 157°	**23** 239°	**24** 317°	**25** 250°

Exercise 55D

Draw each of the following angles.

1 50°	**2** 80°	**3** 45°	**4** 65°	**5** 46°
6 34°	**7** 52°	**8** 85°	**9** 78°	**10** 168°
11 151°	**12** 124°	**13** 203°	**14** 341°	**15** 278°
16 38°	**17** 132°	**18** 223°	**19** 88°	**20** 254°
21 159°	**22** 233°	**23** 163°	**24** 354°	**25** 286°

56/ ACCURATE DRAWINGS

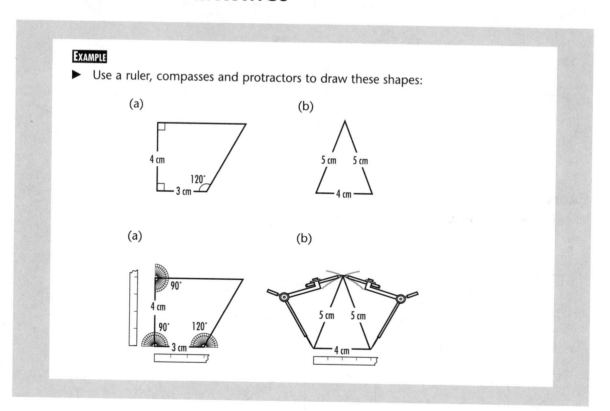

EXAMPLE

▶ Use a ruler, compasses and protractors to draw these shapes:

(a)

(b)

(a)

(b)

Exercise 56A

Draw these shapes accurately using ruler, protractors and, if necessary, compasses.

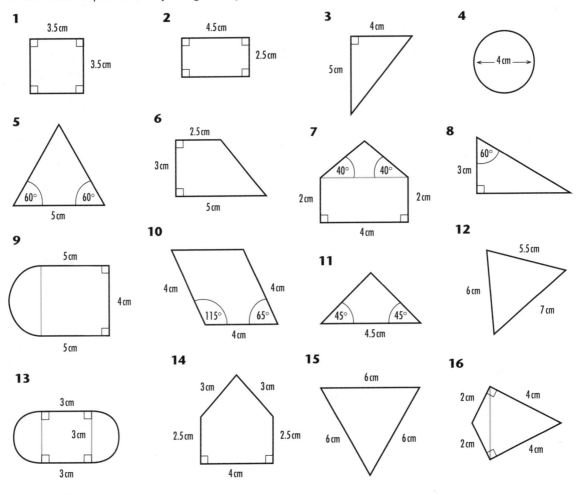

1 3.5 cm 3.5 cm

2 4.5 cm 2.5 cm

3 4 cm 5 cm

4 4 cm

5 60° 60° 5 cm

6 2.5 cm 3 cm 5 cm

7 40° 40° 2 cm 2 cm 4 cm

8 60° 3 cm

9 5 cm 4 cm 5 cm

10 4 cm 4 cm 115° 65° 4 cm

11 45° 45° 4.5 cm

12 5.5 cm 6 cm 7 cm

13 3 cm 3 cm 3 cm

14 3 cm 3 cm 2.5 cm 2.5 cm 4 cm

15 6 cm 6 cm 6 cm

16 2 cm 4 cm 2 cm 4 cm

Exercise 56B

Draw these shapes accurately using ruler, protractors and, if necessary, compasses.

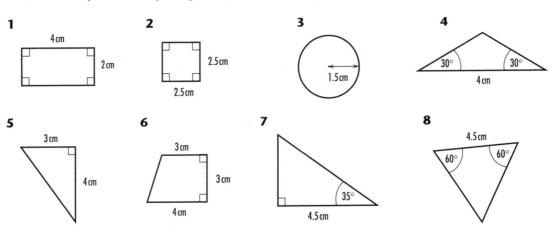

1 4 cm 2 cm

2 2.5 cm 2.5 cm

3 1.5 cm

4 30° 30° 4 cm

5 3 cm 4 cm

6 3 cm 3 cm 4 cm

7 35° 4.5 cm

8 4.5 cm 60° 60°

9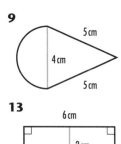
5 cm
4 cm
5 cm

10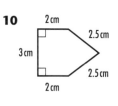
2 cm
2.5 cm
3 cm
2.5 cm
2 cm

11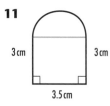
3 cm
3 cm
3.5 cm

12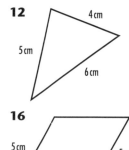
4 cm
5 cm
6 cm

13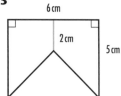
6 cm
2 cm
5 cm

14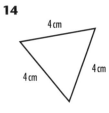
4 cm
4 cm
4 cm

15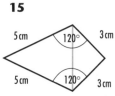
5 cm
120°
3 cm
5 cm
120°
3 cm

16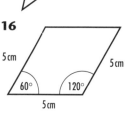
4 cm
5 cm
5 cm
60°
120°
5 cm

57/ CONGRUENT SHAPES

Two shapes are **congruent** if they are identical.

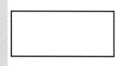

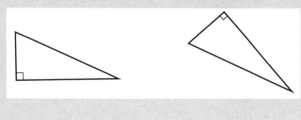

These two shapes are congruent.
The shapes are in different positions but are still congruent.

One rectangle is slighter larger than the other.
They are *not* congruent.

Exercise 57A

Write down whether each pair of shapes is congruent, or not congruent.

1

2

3

4

In each question write down the letters of the two shapes which are congruent.

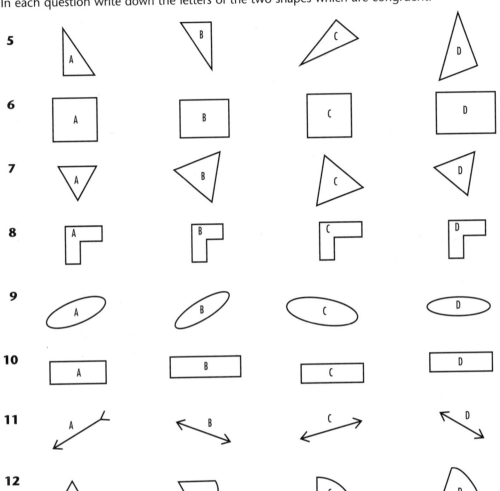

5

6

7

8

9

10

11

12

Copy each shape. Then, for each shape, draw another three which are congruent to the first but in a different position.

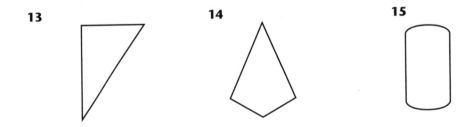

13

14

15

Exercise 57B

Write down whether each pair of shapes is congruent, or not congruent.

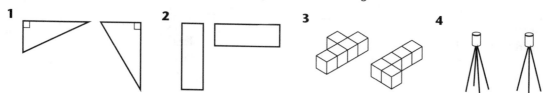

1 **2** **3** **4**

In each question write down the letters of the two shapes which are congruent.

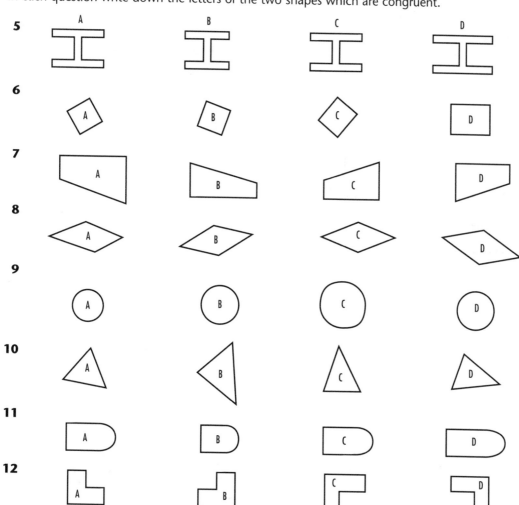

5 A B C D

6 A B C D

7 A B C D

8 A B C D

9 A B C D

10 A B C D

11 A B C D

12 A B C D

Copy each shape. Then, for each shape, draw another three which are congruent to the first but in a different position.

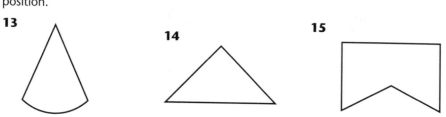

13 **14** **15**

This shape has **reflective symmetry**. The left-hand side is a reflection of the right-hand side.

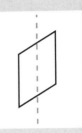

mirror line or line of symmetry

This shape does *not* have reflective symmetry.

EXAMPLE

▶ Copy and complete each diagram by drawing the reflection in the mirror line.

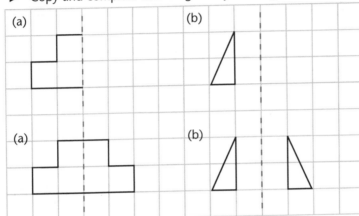

(a)   (b)   (c)

(a)   (b)   (c)

Exercise 58A

Copy and complete each diagram by drawing the reflection in the mirror line(s).

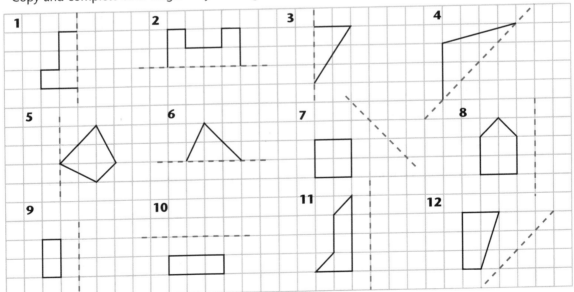

1   2   3   4

5   6   7   8

9   10   11   12

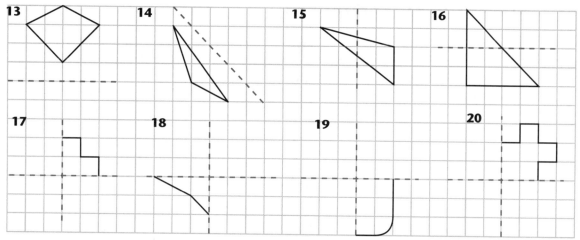

Exercise 58B

Copy and complete each diagram by drawing in the reflection in the mirror line(s).

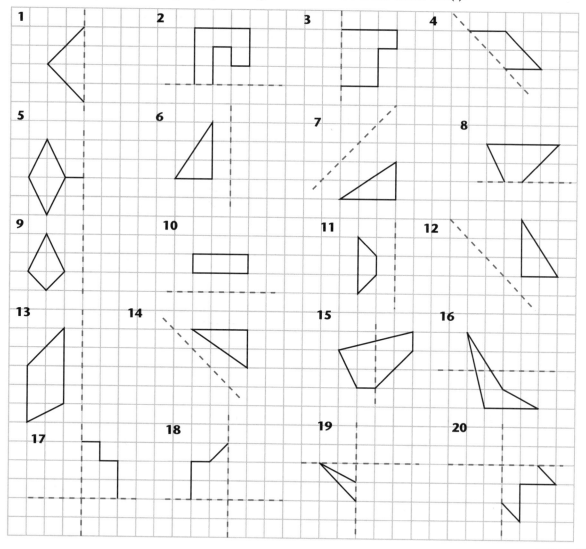

59/ ROTATIONAL SYMMETRY

The number of different ways a shape will fit onto itself is called the **order** of rotation.
A shape has **rotational symmetry** if its order of rotation is greater than 1.
Shape C does *not* have rotational symmetry.

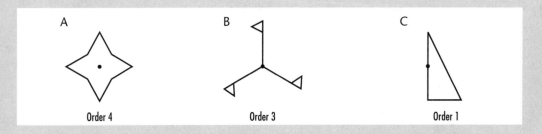

A

B

C

Order 4   Order 3   Order 1

Exercise 59A

(a) Write down the question numbers of the diagrams which do *not* have rotational symmetry.
(b) For those diagrams with rotational symmetry write down the order.

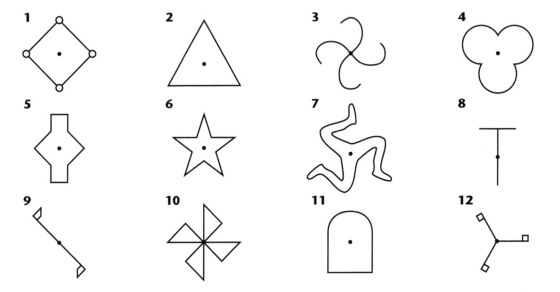

1   2   3   4

5   6   7   8

9   10   11   12

Exercise 59B

(a) Write down the question numbers of the diagrams which do *not* have rotational symmetry.
(b) For those diagrams with rotational symmetry write down the order.

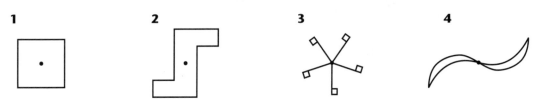

1   2   3   4

5   **6**   **7**   **8**

9   **10**   **11**   **12**

60/ **IDENTIFYING SYMMETRY**

Some shapes have line symmetry *and* rotational symmetry.

EXAMPLE

▶ For this shape state:
(a) the number of lines of symmetry
(b) the order of rotational symmetry.

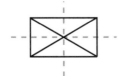

(a) 2   (b) 2

Exercise 60A

For each shape state (a) the number of lines of symmetry (b) the order of rotational symmetry if rotational symmetry exists.

1   **2**   **3**   **4**

5   **6**   **7**   **8**

9   **10**   **11**  **12**

Exercise 60B

For each shape state (a) the number of lines of symmetry (b) the order of rotational symmetry if rotational symmetry exists.

1   **2**   **3**   **4**

5   **6**   **7**   **8**

9    **10**   **11**   **12**

61/ GEOMETRICAL DESCRIPTIONS

Angles are described using special terms:

Acute angle – any angle less than 90°

Obtuse angle – any angle between 90° and 180°

Reflex angle – any angle more than 180°

Right angle – an angle of 90°

Exercise 61A

Give the correct name for each of the following angles.

1 32°	**2** 113°	**3** 203°	**4** 23°	**5** 69°
6 130°	**7** 141°	**8** 18°	**9** 125°	**10** 98°
11 144°	**12** 254°	**13** 342°	**14** 81°	**15** 15°
16 54°	**17** 307°	**18** 230°	**19** 163°	**20** 295°

Exercise 61B

Give the correct name for each of the following angles.

1 10°	**2** 203°	**3** 38°	**4** 344°	**5** 59°
6 139°	**7** 177°	**8** 23°	**9** 120°	**10** 278°
11 97°	**12** 50°	**13** 342°	**14** 154°	**15** 290°
16 20°	**17** 65°	**18** 176°	**19** 44°	**20** 167°

There are several technical terms which are used frequently in geometry to describe common angles or triangles.

Note: The arrows on the lines indicate that the lines are parallel.

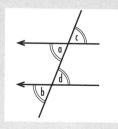

Angles in the positions of *a* and *b* are the same size and are called **corresponding** angles. The angles *c* and *d* are also corresponding.

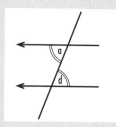

Angles in the position of *a* and *d* are the same size, and are called **alternate** angles.

Angles on a straight line add up to 180°, and are called **supplementary**.

A **right-angled** triangle – a triangle with a right angle
An **equilateral** triangle – a triangle with all three sides the same length (and all three angles 60°)
An **isosceles** triangle – a triangle with two sides the same length and, therefore, two angles the same

Exercise 61C

Give the name of the triangle or the pair of angles indicated.

1

2

3

4

5

6

7
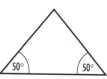

8

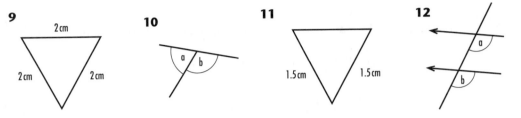

9 2 cm, 2 cm, 2 cm

10 a b

11 1.5 cm, 1.5 cm

12 a b

Exercise 61D

Give the name of the triangle or the pair of angles indicated.

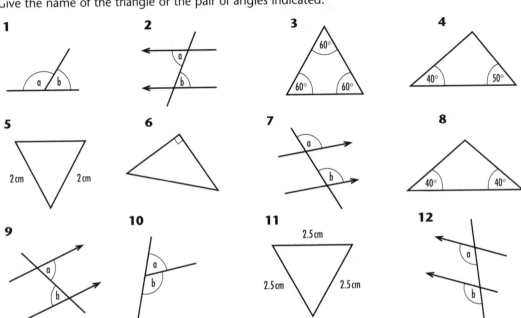

1 a b

2 a b

3 60° 60° 60°

4 40° 50°

5 2 cm 2 cm

6

7 a b

8 40° 40°

9 a b

10 a b

11 2.5 cm, 2.5 cm 2.5 cm

12 a b

REVISION

Exercise E

1 In each question identify the two shapes which are congruent.

(a) W   X   Y   Z

(b) W   X   Y   Z

(c) W   X   Y   Z

(d) W   X   Y   Z

92 SHAPE, SPACE AND MEASURES

2 For each question write down (i) the number of lines of symmetry (ii) the order of rotation.

(a)

(b)

(c)

(d)

(e)

(f)

(g)

(h)

3 Give the correct name to each of the following angles.
(a) 153°   (b) 82°   (c) 39°   (d) 309°   (e) 121°   (f) 224°

4 Give the name of the triangle or the pair of angles indicated in each question.

(a)
3 cm   3 cm
3 cm

(b)

(c)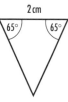
2 cm
65°   65°

(d)

(e)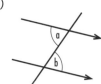
a
b

(f)
2.5 cm   2.5 cm

(g)
60°
60°   60°

(h)
a
b

Exercise EE

1 Measure each of the following angles.

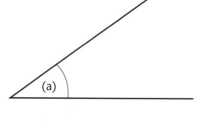
(a)

(b)

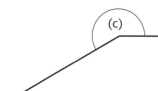
(c)

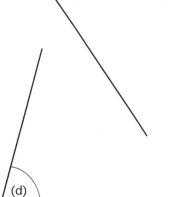
(d)

2 Draw each of the following angles.

(a) 65°   (b) 175°   (c) 260°   (d) 335°   (e) 20°   (f) 130°

3 Draw these shapes accurately using ruler, protractor and compasses as necessary.

(a)

3.8 cm
2.2 cm

(b)
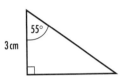
3.5 cm
2.5 cm

(c)

3 cm
40°
6 cm

(d)
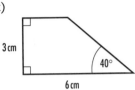
60°   65°
4 cm

(e)
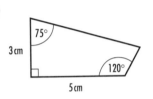
55°
3 cm

(f)
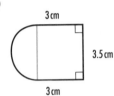
3 cm   120°   3 cm

(g)

4 cm   4 cm
5 cm

(h)

75°
3 cm
120°
5 cm

(i)

3 cm
3.5 cm
3 cm

(j)

5.5 cm
4 cm   5 cm
4.5 cm

4 Copy and complete each diagram by drawing the reflection in the mirror line(s).

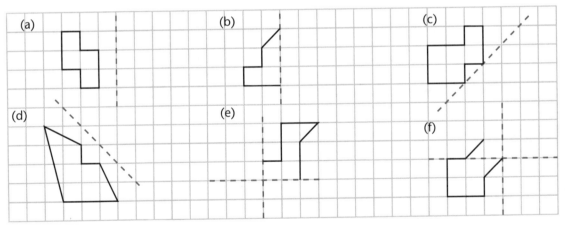

(a)   (b)   (c)   (d)   (e)   (f)

5 Write down the order of rotational symmetry for each diagram.

(a)   (b)   (c)   (d)

(e)

(f)
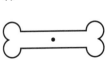

(g)

(h)

Length

1 kilometre (km) = 1000 metres (m)
1 metre (m) = 100 centimetres (cm)
1 metre (m) = 1000 millimetres (mm)
1 centimetre (cm) = 10 millimetres (mm)

Weight

1 kilogram (kg) = 1000 grams (g)
1 gram (g) = 1000 milligrams (mg)
1 tonne (t) = 1000 kilograms (kg)

Capacity

1 litre (*l*) = 100 centilitres (cl)
1 litre (*l*) = 1000 millilitres (ml)
1 centilitre (cl) = 10 millilitres (ml)

To change from one unit into a smaller unit you multiply.
To change from one unit into a larger unit you divide.

EXAMPLE

▶ Change (a) 4.79 kg into grams   (b) 48 cm into metres.

(a) 4.79 kg × 1000 = 4790 g
(b) 48 cm ÷ 100 = 0.48 m

Exercise 62A

Change the following.

1 8 cm into mm	**2** 6 m into cm	**3** 67 m into km	**4** 26.5 mm into cm
5 1350 g into kg	**6** 0.42 *l* into ml	**7** 1.47 kg into g	**8** 1600 ml into cl
9 7 km into m	**10** 153 cm into m	**11** 0.05 *l* into ml	**12** 4 t into kg
13 600 mg into g	**14** 70 cl into *l*	**15** 400 kg into t	**16** 7000 mg into kg
17 0.542 m into cm	**18** 0.05 *l* into ml	**19** 12.41 cm into mm	**20** 4.71 m into cm

Exercise 62B

Change the following.

1 29 m into km	**2** 71.5 mm into cm	**3** 5 cm into mm	**4** 0.84 *l* into ml
5 3 m into cm	**6** 2550 g into kg	**7** 4600 ml into cl	**8** 2.52 kg into g
9 298 cm into m	**10** 0.8 *l* into ml	**11** 6 km into m	**12** 3.5 t into kg
13 250 mg into g	**14** 1.51 cm into mm	**15** 3.03 m into cm	**16** 35 cl into *l*
17 1.49 m into cm	**18** 900 kg into t	**19** 8000 mg into kg	**20** 0.14 *l* into ml

Exercise 62C

1 A man buys 2.3 litres of turpentine, and uses 0.35 litres straight away. The remainder will just fill six bottles. How much will be in each bottle?

2 A car needs 4 litres of oil. A can contains 2.65 litres. How much more oil is needed?

3 A piece of string is 8.64 m long. One third of it is used, and then a second piece 1.29 m long is cut off. What length of string is left?

4 The total mass of three articles is 5 kg. The masses of the first two are 2.74 kg and 1.37 kg. What is the mass of the third article?

5 Saplings are planted 30 cm apart to make a hedge 45 m long. How many saplings are needed?

6 A bottle of orange juice is used to fill eight cups, each of which holds 175 ml. How many litres of orange juice are in the bottle?

7 A lorry load of $2\frac{1}{2}$ tonnes of potatoes is to be shovelled into 2-kg bags. How many bags can be filled from this load?

8 How many 25 g servings of breakfast cereal are there in a box containing 1 kg?

9 If 350 g of minced beef are used in a pie, how many kilograms of minced beef would be needed for 20 pies?

10 A man weighs himself. The scales show 48.5 kg. He then takes off his boots, which weigh 800 g. What weight will now show on the scales?

Exercise 62D

1 A man has two sections of fencing of length 15 m, and two sections of fencing of length 6.5 metres. What is the longest fence that can be built using the four sections?

2 A ferry is loaded with lorries of weight 4 t and 2.75 t, and cars of weight 1 t, 0.95 t and 0.8 t. What is the total weight of vehicles carried on the ferry?

3 A car petrol tank has a capacity of 28 litres. There are 12.5 litres of petrol in the tank. How much more petrol is needed to fill the tank completely?

4 One nail has a mass of 3.55 g. What is the total mass, in kg, of 1200 nails?

5 How many pieces of string can be cut from a five-metre length if each piece is 15 cm long?

6 A small bottle holds 75 ml of liquid. How many litres of liquid will be required to fill 1000 small bottles?

7 A woman is running a 5-km race. She has already run 1450 m. How many metres has she yet to run?

8 Dipak has used 200 g of flour in making a cake, and 75 g in making buns. How much flour will be left if he started with a 5-kg bag?

9 One ball-bearing has a mass of 23 g. What will be the mass, in kg, of 2500 ball-bearings?

10 A snail covers a distance of 6 cm in a minute. If it continues at the same speed, what is the maximum distance it could cover in eight hours? Give your answer in metres.

63/ SENSIBLE ESTIMATES

Exercise 63A

For each question write down the letter of the estimate which best matches the statement.

1 The height of a door   2 The weight of an adult
3 The length of an index finger 4 The width of a double bed

5 The height of a lamp post   **6** The weight of a text book

7 The length of a pen   **8** The capacity of an egg cup

9 The length of a family car   **10** The weight of a car

11 The weight of a bag of sugar   **12** The length of an ant

13 The capacity of a can of fizzy drink   **14** The distance from Newcastle to London

15 The capacity of a bottle of wine   **16** The weight of an exercise book

17 The height of Mount Everest   **18** The capacity of a milk pan

19 The distance across a town   **20** The weight of a bag of concrete

A 75 cl	**B** 8 m	**C** 1 kg	**D** 75 kg	**E** 0.8 *l*
F 3 mm	**G** 1.5 m	**H** 30 kg	**I** 330 ml	**J** 2 m
K 40 ml	**L** 20 g	**M** 7 cm	**N** 400 g	**O** 8848 m
P 15 km	**Q** 15 cm	**R** 4.4 m	**S** 444 km	**T** 1 t

Exercise 63B

For each question write down the letter of the estimate which best matches the statement.

1 The length of a new-born baby.   **2** The weight of a £1 coin

3 The distance from Leeds to London   **4** The capacity of a tea pot

5 The height of a house   **6** The weight of a large tin of beans

7 The height of Snowdon   **8** The capacity of a milk bottle

9 The length of a classroom   **10** The capacity of a tea cup

11 The weight of an iron   **12** The diameter of a standard music CD

13 The capacity of a washing-up bowl   **14** The width of a family car

15 The amount of fluid in a teaspoon   **16** The height of a dining-room table

17 The capacity of a garden pond   **18** The width of the screen on a portable TV

19 The distance around the equator   **20** The distance from London to Paris

A 200 ml	**B** 420 g	**C** 75 cm	**D** 12700 km	**E** 10 g
F 550 ml	**G** 1 kg	**H** 5000 *l*	**I** 340 km	**J** 328 km
K 49 cm	**L** 1 *l*	**M** 30 cm	**N** 12 cm	**O** 10 m
P 1085 m	**Q** 5 ml	**R** 8 m	**S** 10 *l*	**T** 1.7 m

Length

    1 mile = 1760 yards (yd)
    1 yard (yd) = 3 feet (ft)
    1 foot (ft) = 12 inches (in)

Capacity

    1 gallon (gal) = 8 pints (pt)
    1 pint (pt) = 20 fluid ounces (fl. oz)

Weight

    1 ton = 20 hundredweight (cwt)
    1 hundredweight (cwt) = 112 pounds (lb)
    1 pound (lb) = 16 ounces (oz)
    1 stone (st) = 14 pounds (lb)

EXAMPLE

▶ Change   (a) 2 ft 8 in into in   (b) 70 in into ft and in

           (c) $7\frac{1}{2}$ yd into ft   (d) 22 ft into yd and ft.

(a) 2 ft 8 in = $(2 \times 12) + 8 = 32$ inches   (b) 70 in = $(5 \times 12) + 10 = 5$ ft 10 in

(c) $7\frac{1}{2}$ yd = $(7\frac{1}{2} \times 3) = 22\frac{1}{2}$ ft   (d) 22 ft = $(7 \times 3) + 1 = 7$ yd 1 ft

Exercise 64A

Change the following.

1 $73\frac{1}{2}$ in into ft and in	**2** $3\frac{1}{2}$ yd into ft	**3** 125 lb into st and lb
4 4 lb 3 oz into oz	**5** $1\frac{3}{4}$ gal into pt	**6** 1 mile 39 yd into yd
7 $\frac{3}{4}$ lb into oz	**8** 70 in into ft and in	**9** 65 in into ft and in
10 3 yd 2 ft into ft	**11** $\frac{5}{8}$ mile into yd	**12** 200 lb into st and lb
13 3 yd 1 ft into ft	**14** 3 ft 11 in into in	**15** 3 lb 3 oz into oz
16 $\frac{1}{4}$ yd into in	**17** 25 ft into yd and ft	**18** $\frac{1}{4}$ pt into fl. oz
19 52 st into cwt	**20** $34\frac{1}{4}$ in into ft and in	

Exercise 64B

Change the following.

1 48 in into ft	**2** 25 pt into gal and pt	**3** 3000 yd into miles and yd
4 12 ft 3 in into in	**5** 115 lb into st and lb	**6** 3 ft 4 in into in
7 10 st 5 lb into lb	**8** 3 pt into fl. oz	**9** $6\frac{1}{4}$ ft into in
10 7 yd 1 ft into ft	**11** 3 tons 4 cwt into cwt	**12** 4 ft 5 in into in

13 $\frac{3}{4}$ pt into fl. oz　　　**14** 4 yd 1 ft into ft　　　**15** $4\frac{1}{4}$ lb into oz

16 $\frac{3}{4}$ yd into in　　　**17** $2\frac{1}{4}$ gal into pt　　　**18** 7 ft 4 in into in

19 50 in into ft and in　　　**20** 3 miles 400 yd into yd

Exercise 64C

1 A heavyweight boxer weighs 224 lb. How many stones is this?

2 A gardener has three bags of fertiliser with weights of 6 lb 8 oz, 2 lb 12 oz, and 14 lb 4 oz. How much has he altogether?

3 A man is 5 ft $8\frac{1}{2}$ in tall. His daughter is 4 ft $11\frac{1}{2}$ in tall. Find the difference in their heights.

4 A length of rope is 9 ft 3 in long. A length of 6 ft 7 in is cut off. How much is left?

5 A block of cheese, which weighs 3 lb 9 oz, is to be divided into twelve equal portions. How many ounces will each portion weigh?

6 It takes 9 lb 8 oz of flour to make four cakes. How much flour will be needed for just one cake?

7 A rectangle has a length of 2 yd 2 ft, and a width of 1 yd 2 ft. Find the total distance around the edge of the rectangle.

8 A can has a capacity of 1 gal 3 pt. What is the total capacity of ten similar cans?

9 How many pint bottles can be filled from a five-gallon milk churn?

10 A man weighed 15 st 7 lb. He lost 3 st 10 lb. What does he now weigh?

Exercise 64D

1 A can has a capacity of 5 gal 4 pt. What is the total capacity of six similar cans?

2 A length of curtain measures 6 ft 10 in. It also has a folded hem of 6 in. What is the total length of the fabric in the curtain?

3 Two boxes of weight 4 lb 8 oz and 5 lb 12 oz are put into the boot of a car. What is the total weight of the two boxes?

4 A bag contains 9 lb 9 oz of sand. Sand of weight 5 lb 11 oz is removed. How much sand is left?

5 A petrol tank is filled to a capacity of 12 gal. How many gallons and pints will be left in the tank if 5 gal 7 pt of petrol are then used in a journey?

6 The width of a plot of land is 8 yd 2 ft. What is the distance across six such adjacent plots of land?

7 Twelve lengths of telephone cable, each 65 ft long, are hung on poles from one end of a road to the other. What is the total length of the road?

8 An athlete drinks $1\frac{1}{4}$ pt of milk each day. How many gallons will the athlete drink in twelve weeks?

9 Eight copies of the same textbook are stacked. The total height of the stack is 3 ft 6 in. What is the width of each book?

10 A tank holds 4 gal 3 pt of liquid. If 1 gal 7 pt is taken out of the tank, what amount of liquid is left?

65/ METRIC AND IMPERIAL EQUIVALENTS

When comparing quantities in metric and Imperial units, two quantities which are approximately the same are said to be equivalent (≈).

The following are common metric and Imperial equivalents:

5 miles ≈ 8 kilometres

1 foot ≈ 30 centimetres

1 kilogram ≈ 2.2 pounds

1 yard ≈ 1 metre

1 inch ≈ 2.5 centimetres

1 litre ≈ 1.75 pints

> **EXAMPLE**
> ▶ Change (a) 60 miles into kilometre (b) 32 kilometres into miles.
>
> (a) 60 miles ≈ $60 \times \frac{8}{5} = \frac{480}{5} = 96$ km
>
> (b) 32 km ≈ $32 \times \frac{5}{8} = \frac{160}{8} = 20$ miles

Exercise 65A

Change the following into their approximate equivalents.

1 20 kg into lb	**2** 12 in into cm	**3** 10 miles into km	**4** 15.75 pt into l
5 19.8 lb into kg	**6** 8 l into pt	**7** 3 ft into cm	**8** 16 km into miles
9 35 miles into km	**10** $3\frac{1}{2}$ yd into m	**11** 44 km into miles	**12** $3\frac{1}{2}$ gal into l
13 75 cm into ft	**14** 23.1 lb into kg	**15** 25 cm into in	**16** 7 ft into cm
17 20 l into pt	**18** 5 m into yd	**19** 12.5 cm into in	**20** 50 kg into lb

Exercise 65B

Change the following into their approximate equivalents.

1 20 miles into kg	**2** 30 kg into lb	**3** 4 ft into cm	**4** 7 gal into l
5 18 in into cm	**6** 32 km into miles	**7** 13.2 lb into kg	**8** 22.75 pt into l
9 12 l into pt	**10** $7\frac{1}{2}$ yd into m	**11** 45 cm into ft	**12** 35 cm into in
13 8 ft into cm	**14** 36 in into cm	**15** 34.1 lb into kg	**16** 60 km into miles
17 6.5 m into yd	**18** 16 l into pt	**19** 15 cm into in	**20** 45 miles into km

Exercise 65C

Find the approximate equivalent in each question.

1 A pair of trousers has a waist measurement of 36 inches. What is this in centimetres?

2 A window is 6 ft high. What is its height in metres?

3 Which is heavier: (a) a 4-kg packet of sugar or (b) a 5-lb bag of potatoes?

4 A scuba-diver carries ten lead weights, each weighing $\frac{1}{4}$ lb, in his belt. His air-tank weighs 5 kg. What is the total weight of his equipment, in kg?

5 If 250 g of flour is needed in a recipe, what is this in ounces?

6 A salesman drives 332 km in one day. How many miles is this?

7 A driver buys 30 litres of petrol. How many gallons is this?

8 An instruction in a knitting pattern indicates a measurement of 6 inches. What is this in centimetres?

9 The distance between Calais and Paris is about 270 km. What is this in miles?

10 A tank contains 45 gallons of water. How many litres is this?

Exercise 65D

Find the approximate equivalent in each question.

1 A roll of carpet is 12 yards long. What is this in metres?

2 A Christmas hamper weighs 8 kg. What is its weight in pounds?

3 In adjacent shops they are selling (a) 3 kg of potatoes for 80p (b) 5 lb of potatoes for the same price. Which is the better buy?

4 A house is estimated to be 28 ft high. How high is this in metres?

5 A man is 1.8 metres tall. What is his height in feet?

6 A recipe requires 0.4 kg of flour. How many ounces is this?

7 The distance between London and Dover is 70 miles. What is this in km?

8 A driver buys 40 litres of petrol. How many gallons is this?

9 A length of fabric measures 95 inches. What is this in centimetres?

10 A path has been laid. Its length is 30 feet. What is this in metres?

66/ SCALES

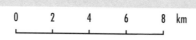

This scale measures 4 cm and represents 8 km. The scale is 4 cm to 8 km, or 1 cm to 2 km.

0.5 cm represents 1 km.

4.2 cm represents 8.4 km.

Exercise 66A

In each question give the distance represented by the measurement on the scale.

1 0 10 20 30 40 km (a) 1.0 cm (b) 2.5 cm (c) 3.2 cm (d) 0.8 cm

2 0 100 200 300 400 m (a) 3.0 cm (b) 0.4 cm (c) 1.7 cm (d) 3.6 cm

3 0 20 40 60 80 km (a) 2.0 cm (b) 2.8 cm (c) 1.4 cm (d) 3.5 cm

4 0 4 8 12 16 m   (a) 4.0 cm (b) 1.2 cm (c) 2.4 cm (d) 3.8 cm

5 0 6 12 18 24 m   (a) 1.0 cm (b) 2.2 cm (c) 3.4 cm (d) 0.7 cm

6 0 5 10 15 20 km   (a) 4.0 cm (b) 0.6 cm (c) 1.9 cm (d) 2.3 cm

7 0 30 60 90 120 m   (a) 3.0 cm (b) 0.5 cm (c) 2.9 cm (d) 3.7 cm

8 0 25 50 75 100 km   (a) 2.0 cm (b) 3.9 cm (c) 1.5 cm (d) 0.3 cm

Exercise 66B

In each question give the distance represented by the measurement on the scale.

1 0 10 20 30 40 km   (a) 3.0 cm (b) 0.2 cm (c) 2.1 cm (d) 3.6 cm

2 0 4 8 12 16 km   (a) 2.0 cm (b) 1.5 cm (c) 2.6 cm (d) 3.3 cm

3 0 5 10 15 20 m   (a) 4.0 cm (b) 0.1 cm (c) 1.6 cm (d) 2.7 cm

4 0 20 40 60 80 km   (a) 1.0 cm (b) 3.1 cm (c) 2.8 cm (d) 2.2 cm

5 0 25 50 75 100 m   (a) 2.0 cm (b) 0.9 cm (c) 3.1 cm (d) 1.6 cm

6 0 8 16 24 32 m   (a) 1.0 cm (b) 2.4 cm (c) 2.9 cm (d) 3.7 cm

7 0 150 300 450 600 km   (a) 3.0 cm (b) 1.1 cm (c) 2.4 cm (d) 3.5 cm

8 0 70 140 210 280 m   (a) 4.0 cm (b) 0.4 cm (c) 1.8 cm (d) 3.2 cm

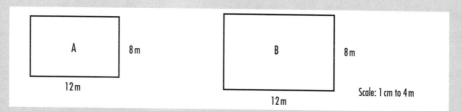

The dimensions shown in Diagram A are actual measurements.
A **scale** is used to draw an accurate diagram of the dimensions but to a smaller size than the original measurements.
Diagram B shows how the scale diagram looks, using a scale of 1 cm to 4 m.
Note: The actual (larger) dimensions are written on the scale diagram.

Exercise 66C

Draw scale diagrams for the following dimensions using the scale stated in each question.

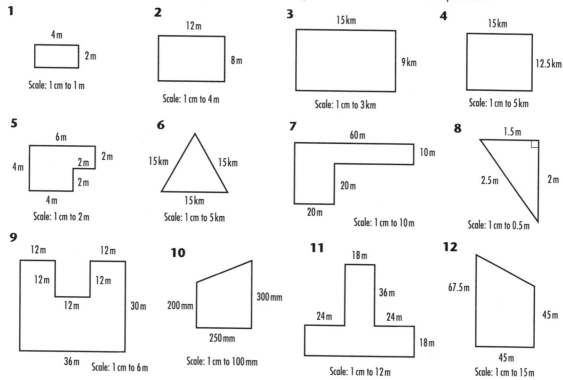

In each case draw the shape to scale and measure the length of the missing side. Use your scale to give the measurement its actual length.

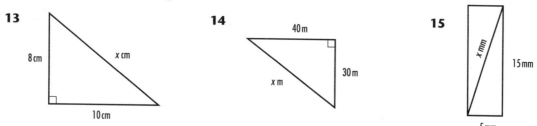

Exercise 66D

Draw scale diagrams for the following dimensions using the scale stated in each question.

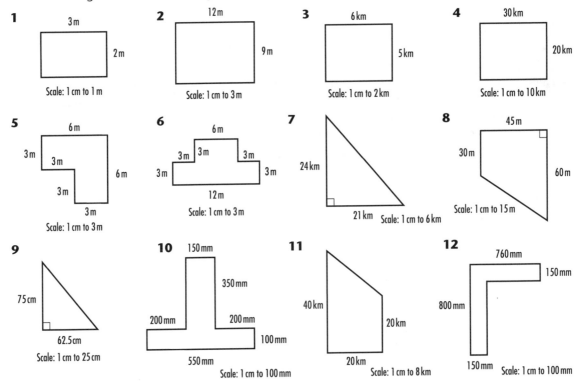

1
3m
2m
Scale: 1 cm to 1 m

2
12m
9m
Scale: 1 cm to 3 m

3
6km
5km
Scale: 1 cm to 2 km

4
30km
20km
Scale: 1 cm to 10 km

5
6m
3m
3m
6m
3m
3m
Scale: 1 cm to 3 m

6
6m
3m 3m 3m
3m
3m
12m
Scale: 1 cm to 3 m

7
24km
21km
Scale: 1 cm to 6 km

8
45m
30m
60m
Scale: 1 cm to 15 m

9
75cm
62.5cm
Scale: 1 cm to 25 cm

10
150mm
350mm
200mm
200mm
100mm
550mm
Scale: 1 cm to 100 mm

11
40km
20km
20km
Scale: 1 cm to 8 km

12
760mm
150mm
800mm
150mm
Scale: 1 cm to 100 mm

In each case draw the shape to scale and measure the length of the missing side. Use your scale to give the measurement its actual length.

13
1.5km
2.5km
x km

14
20km
x km
25km

15
x mm
350mm
400mm

67/ AREA AND PERIMETER

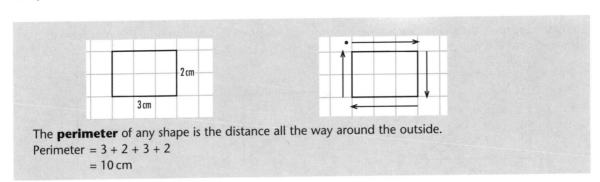

2cm

3cm

The **perimeter** of any shape is the distance all the way around the outside.
Perimeter = 3 + 2 + 3 + 2
       = 10 cm

The **area** of any shape is a measure of the surface contained within it.
Area = 6 cm^2

The perimeter is a length, and is measured in mm, cm, m, km etc.
The area is a measure of surface, and is measured in mm^2, cm^2, m^2, km^2 etc.

Exercise 67A

Find (a) the perimeter (b) the area of each shape (1 square represents 1cm^2).

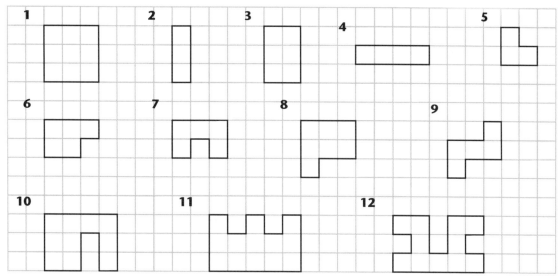

Draw these diagrams on a squared grid to help you find (a) the perimeter (b) the area of each shape.

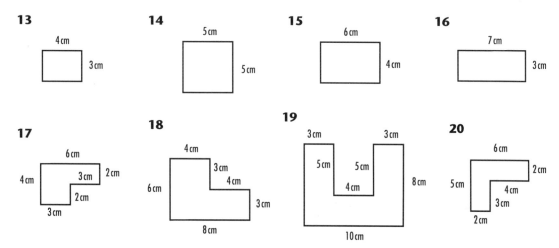

Exercise 67B

Find (a) the perimeter (b) the area of each shape (1 square represents 1cm²).

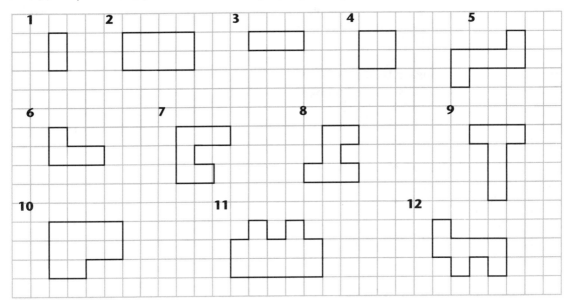

Draw these diagrams on a squared grid to help you find (a) the perimeter (b) the area of each shape.

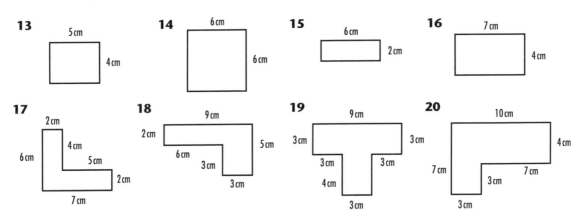

68/ VOLUME

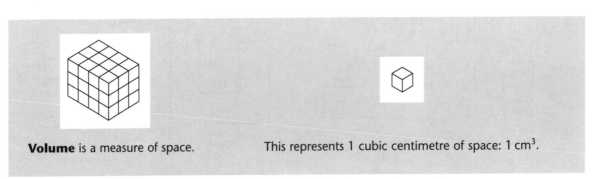

Volume is a measure of space.

This represents 1 cubic centimetre of space: 1 cm³.

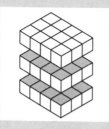

Each layer of this space contains 12 cm³.
But there are three layers, so the
total volume   = 12 + 12 + 12
            = 36 cm³.

Exercise 68A

Find the volume, in cm³, of each of these solids.

1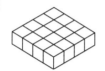

2

3

4

5

6

7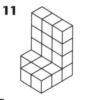

8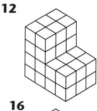

9

10

11

12

13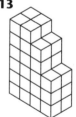

14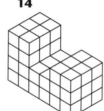

15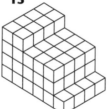

16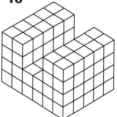

Exercise 68B

Find the volume, in cm³, of each of these solids.

1

2

3

4

5

6

7

8

9 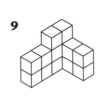   **10**   **11**   **12**

13 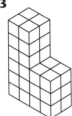   **14** 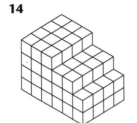   **15** 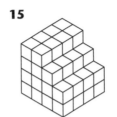   **16**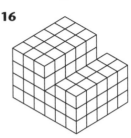

REVISION

Exercise F

1 Change the following:

   (a) 3 km into m   (b) 45 g into kg   (c) 4.78 t into kg   (d) 400 mg into g

   (e) 150 kg into t   (f) 632 cm into m   (g) 184 m into km   (h) 0.03 m into mm

   (i) 80 cl into *l*   (j) 6.5 m into cm   (k) 4300 ml into cl

2 Change the following:

   (a) 0.73 *l* into ml   (b) 3 g into mg   (c) 50 cwt into tons and cwt

   (d) 155 lb into st and lb   (e) 40 pt into gal   (f) 38 oz into lb and oz

   (g) 427 ml into *l*   (h) 4 lb 5 oz into oz   (i) 30 000 yd into miles and yd

   (j) 130 lb into cwt and lb   (k) 125 in into ft and in   (l) 1 cwt 50 lb into lb

3 Change the following:

   (a) 40 ft into yd and ft   (b) $4\frac{3}{4}$ gal into pt   (c) 24 *l* into gal   (d) 64 km into miles

   (e) 50 kg into lb   (f) 35 pt into *l*   (g) 150 miles into km   (h) 96 in into cm

   (i) 110 lb into kg   (j) $2\frac{1}{2}$ yd into cm   (k) 66 lb into kg   (l) 56 *l* into gal

4 In each question give the real distance represented by the distance on the scale.

   (a)

          0   10   20   30   40 km

         (i) 3.0 cm   (ii) 1.7 cm   (iii) 2.3 cm   (iv) 0.8 cm

   (b)

          0   8   16   24   32 m

         (i) 2.0 cm   (ii) 0.5 cm   (iii) 3.7 cm   (iv) 2.6 cm

   (c)

          0   250   500   750   1000 mm

         (i) 1.0 cm   (ii) 3.5 cm   (iii) 2.8 cm   (iv) 1.4 cm

5 Draw scale diagrams for the following measurements using the scale stated in each question.

(a)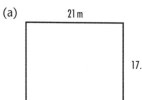

21 m

17.5 m

Scale: 1 cm to 7 m

(b)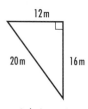

12 m

20 m   16 m

Scale: 1 cm to 4 m

(c)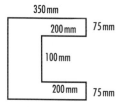

350 mm

200 mm   75 mm

100 mm

200 mm   75 mm

Scale: 1 cm to 50 mm

6 Find (i) the perimeter (ii) the area of each shape.

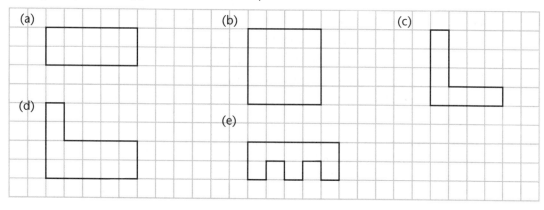

7 Find the volume of each shape.

 = 1 cm³

(a)

(b)

(c)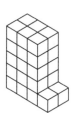

(d)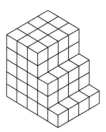

Exercise FF

1 Three pieces of wood are of lengths 3 m, 42 cm and 320 cm. If these are placed end to end, what will be their total length, in metres?

2 What is the total weight, in kg, of three packets which weigh 2 kg, 460 g and 480 g.

3 A lorry has a load of weight 0.8 tonnes. A 52-kg bag of cement is taken off the lorry. What weight, in kg, is the remainder of the load?

4 Find the total length, in metres, of a piece of string 84 cm long, and another piece of string 360 mm long.

5 A tin of beans weighs 420 g. What is the weight, in kg, of eight of these tins?

6 A small bottle has a capacity of 55 ml. How many litres of fluid is needed to fill 500 small bottles?

7 A man weighs $12\frac{1}{2}$ stone. He loses 21 lb whilst on a diet. How much will he now weigh?

8 A furlong is $\frac{1}{8}$ of a mile. A horse has run 5 furlongs. How many yards is this?

9 A farmer has three buckets which hold 4 gal 4 pt, 2 gal 5 pt and 2 gal 6 pt of milk. How much milk is there altogether?

10 A bag of coal weighs 1 cwt. If 25 bags are loaded onto a lorry, what is the weight of the load, in tons and cwt?

11 A length of wire 8 yards long is cut into three equal pieces. What is the length of each piece of wire?

12 A tank contains 6 gal 5 pt of liquid. A further 1 gal 5 pt is added to the tank. How much liquid is there now in the tank?

13 What is the chest size, in inches, of a jumper marked at 105 cm?

14 A woman is 1.6 metres tall. What is her height in feet and inches?

15 A large box weighs 440 lb. What is its weight in kilogram?

16 A tank contains 40 gallons of water. Then 54 litres is siphoned out. How many gallons of water remain?

17 A man has a weight of 18 st 10 lb. He loses 53 kg in weight. What is his new weight, in st and lb?

18 Three pieces of wood of length 42 inches, $2\frac{1}{2}$ feet and 1.4 metres are placed end to end. What is the total length, in metres?

19 A ladder leans against a wall. The foot of the ladder is 3.5 m from the wall. The ladder is 6.5 m in length. Draw a scale diagram, and use the diagram to find the height of the top of the ladder above the ground.

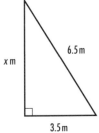

20 A yard is 15 m wide and 20 m across. Draw a scale diagram of the yard, and use the diagram to find the distance from one corner of the yard to the opposite corner.

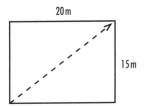

21 This is the floor plan of an office.

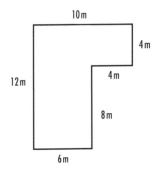

(a) What is the perimeter of the office?

(b) The manager plans to tile the floor with carpet tiles which measure 1 metre square. How many tiles will be needed?

(c) The manager is also thinking about carpeting the floor with larger carpet squares which are 2 m × 2 m in dimension.
   (i) Draw a scale diagram of the office floor.
   (ii) Draw lines on your scale diagram to show how the 2 m × 2 m carpet squares would be laid.
   (iii) How many carpet squares would be needed?

Handling data

69/ INTERPRETING DIAGRAMS

Exercise 69A

Use the information shown in each graph to answer the questions.

1 (a) Which score was thrown the most?

(b) Which score was thrown the least?

(c) Which two scores were thrown an equal number of times?

(d) How many times was the dice thrown?

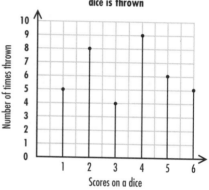

Graph of the number of times each score on a dice is thrown

2 (a) What was the value of the car in (i) 1997 (ii) 2000 (iii) 2003?

(b) Between which two years was there the greatest fall in value?

(c) What is the fall in value between (i) 1998 and 2000 (ii) 1999 and 2003?

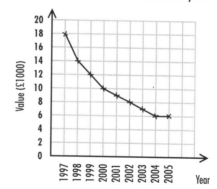

Graph of the value of a car over several years

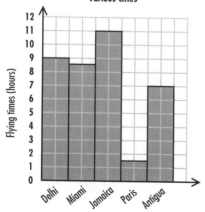

Graph of the flying times from London to various cities

3 (a) Which destination has the longest flying time?

(b) Which destination has the shortest flying time?

(c) How long does it take to get to (i) Miami (ii) Antigua?

Graph showing the weights of packets

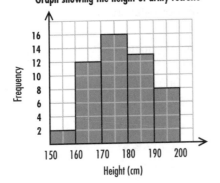

4 (a) How many packets weighed between
(i) 250 g and 300 g (ii) 200 g and 250 g?

(b) Between which two weights were there
exactly 6 packets?

(c) Between which two weights were there the
most packets?

5 (a) What percentage unemployment was
recorded in (i) March (ii) July
(iii) December?

(b) In which month was the percentage
unemployment (i) 55% (ii) 70%?

(c) State the percentage and the month in
which the highest unemployment was
recorded.

**Graph showing the percentage of people unemployed
throughout one year**

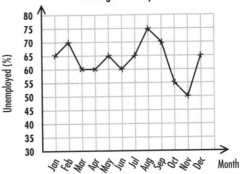

Graph of the number of pairs of shoes sold during one day

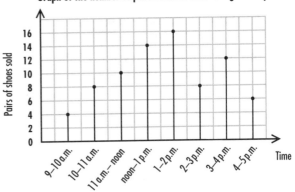

6 (a) What was the maximum number of
pairs of shoes sold in one hour?

(b) Between which two times was the
smallest number of shoes sold?

(c) During which times were eight
pairs of shoes sold?

Graph showing the height of army recruits

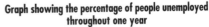

7 (a) How many recruits had a height between
(i) 180 cm and 190 cm
(ii) 160 cm and 180 cm?

(b) Between which two heights were there
exactly eight recruits?

(c) Between which two heights was there the
smallest number of recruits?

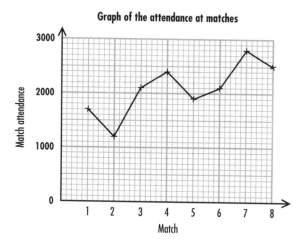

Graph of the attendance at matches

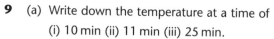

8 (a) Write down the match attendance at
(i) match 3 (ii) match 5 (iii) match 8.

(b) Which two matches had the same attendance?

(c) What was the (i) highest attendance (ii) lowest attendance?

9 (a) Write down the temperature at a time of
(i) 10 min (ii) 11 min (iii) 25 min.

(b) Write down the times at which the temperature was 15°C.

(c) State the time and temperature at the points of the graph which are
(i) highest (ii) lowest.

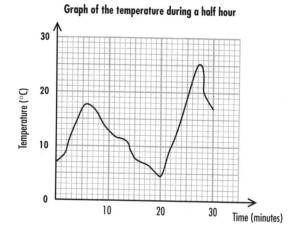

Graph of the temperature during a half hour

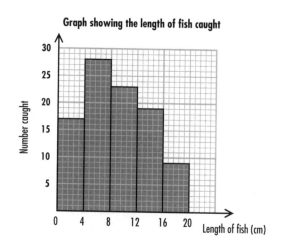

Graph showing the length of fish caught

10 (a) How many fishes were caught with a length between 12 cm and 16 cm?

(b) How many fishes were caught with a length under (i) 8 cm (ii) 12 cm?

(c) How many fishes were caught with a length of more than 12 cm?

Exercise 69B

Use the information shown in each graph to answer the questions.

1 (a) Which channel was selected the most?
 (b) Which channel was selected the least?
 (c) Which channel was selected five times?
 (d) What is the total number of channel selections made?

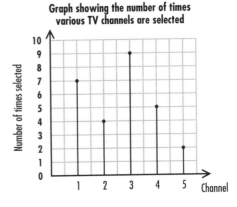

Graph showing the number of times various TV channels are selected

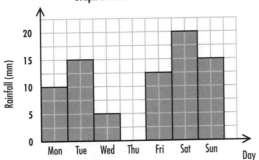

Graph of the rainfall in one week

2 (a) On which day was there the most rainfall?
 (b) How much rainfall was there on
 (i) Monday (ii) Friday?
 (c) Which two days had the same rainfall?
 (d) Which day of the week was dry?

3 (a) In which year was the least profit?
 (b) Which years had a profit of £14m?
 (c) Write down the profit in years
 (i) 1986 (ii) 1992 (iii) 1996.

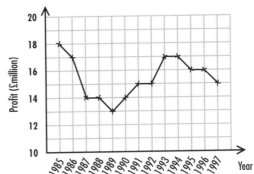

Graph of a company's profit over several years

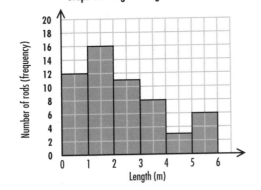

Graph showing the length of metal rods

4 (a) How many rods have a length between
 (i) 2 m and 3 m (ii) 5 m and 6 m?
 (b) Between which lengths are there the most rods?
 (c) How many rods have a length of less than 3 m?

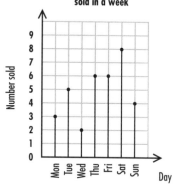

Graph of the number of televisions sold in a week

5 (a) On which day were the most televisions sold?

(b) On which two days was the same number of televisions sold?

(c) How many televisions were sold on
(i) Wednesday (ii) Sunday?

6 (a) What was the smallest attendance at the tournament?

(b) On which two days was the attendance the same?

(c) What was the attendance on (i) Day 5 (ii) Day 7?

(d) What was the greatest increase in the attendance from one day to the next?

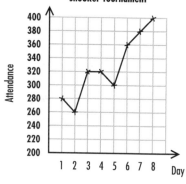

Graph showing the attendance at a snooker tournament

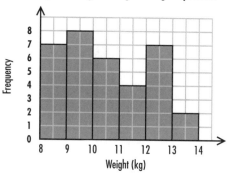

Graph showing the weight of bags of potatoes

7 (a) How many bags of potatoes weighed between (i) 8 kg and 9 kg (ii) 11 kg and 12 kg?

(b) Between which two weights was there the greatest number of bags?

(c) How many bags had a weight greater than (i) 12 kg (ii) 10 kg?

8 (a) What was the cost of the telephone calls made during (i) Week 2 (ii) Week 7?

(b) During which weeks were telephone calls made costing (i) £24 (ii) £44?

(c) What was the greatest fall in telephone costs between two consecutive weeks?

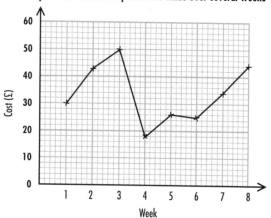

Graph of the cost of telephone calls made over several weeks

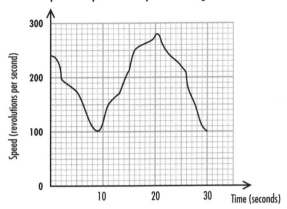

Graph of the speed of an object over a length of time

9 (a) What was the speed at a time of
(i) 11 seconds (ii) 23 seconds?

(b) At what times was the recorded speed 170 rev/s?

(c) Write down the (i) maximum speed (ii) minimum speed recorded.

10 (a) Between which two capacities did 27 stores record sales of oil?

(b) How many stores recorded sales between (i) 10 *l* and 20 *l* (ii) 40 *l* and 50 *l*?

(c) How many stores recorded sales of (i) under 30 *l* (ii) over 30 *l*?

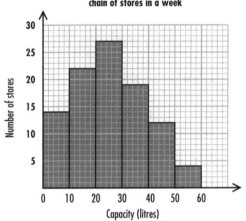

Graph showing the amount of oil sold in a chain of stores in a week

70/ DRAWING BAR LINE GRAPHS

EXAMPLE

▶ Show the data in the table as a bar line graph.

Dice	1	2	3	4	5	6
Frequency	8	4	5	4	6	5

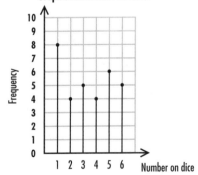

Graph of the scores on a dice

Exercise 70A

Draw a bar line graph for each of the following tables.

1

Score on dice	1	2	3	4	5	6
Frequency	4	7	6	4	5	5

2

Coins	1p	2p	3p	4p	5p	6p
Frequency	4	7	10	8	3	5

3

Birds	Sparrow	Tit	Thrush	Swallow
Frequency	11	8	4	5

4

Day	Mon.	Tue.	Wed.	Thu.	Fri.
Late buses	10	7	5	8	7

5

Pupils	Susan	Ali	Remi	Vera	Ben
Frequency	18	10	16	11	15

6

Tree	Oak	Ash	Beech	Elm	Birch
Frequency	3	10	7	8	15

7

Day	Mon.	Tue.	Wed.	Thu.	Fri.	Sat.
Hours worked	6	8	8	9	10	4

8

Month	J	F	M	A	M	J	J	A
Sunny days	15	12	8	10	15	16	22	18

Exercise 70B

Draw a bar line graph for each of the following tables.

1

Passengers in cars	1	2	3	4	5
Frequency	10	7	8	4	3

2

Colour of car	Red	Blue	Brown	Black	White	Green	Other
Frequency	8	11	6	4	2	3	9

3

Child	Josie	Chris	Katy	John	Ruth
Presents	7	8	14	16	5

4	Day	Mon.	Tue.	Wed.	Thu.	Fri.
	Coffees drunk	7	6	9	8	4

5	Year	1994	1995	1996	1997	1998	1999
	Train journeys	15	23	20	17	18	21

6	Week	1	2	3	4	5	6	7	8
	Test mark (%)	84	73	85	64	82	77	97	78

7	Day born on	Mon.	Tue.	Wed.	Thu.	Fri.	Sat.	Sun.
	Frequency	21	33	24	36	29	37	24

8	Competition points	5	10	20	50	100	200
	Frequency	27	35	32	24	26	18

71/ DRAWING LINE GRAPHS

EXAMPLE

▶ Show the data in the table as a line graph.

Month	Jan.	Feb.	Mar.	Apr.	May.	Jun.
Late deliveries	5	4	3	6	7	8

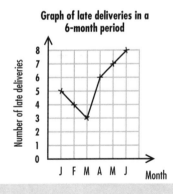

Graph of late deliveries in a 6-month period

Exercise 71A

Draw a line graph for each of the following tables.

1	Day	Mon.	Tue.	Wed.	Thu.	Fri.
	Fireworks made	28	34	35	32	26

2

Time	7 a.m.	9 a.m.	11 a.m.	1 p.m.	3 p.m.	5 p.m.
Temperature (°F)	50	70	65	70	74	61

3

Month	Jan.	Feb.	Mar.	Apr.	May	Jun.	Jul.	Aug.
Profit (£m)	4	7	8	6	5	7	10	14

4

Miles travelled	1	2	3	4	5	6
Speed (m.p.h.)	50	45	48	30	42	58

5

Year	1995	1996	1997	1998	1999	2000	2001	2002
Value	£400	£420	£390	£365	£350	£340	£332	£329

6

Lesson	1	2	3	4	5	6	7	8
Lines of writing	32	20	5	12	40	34	42	40

7

Day	Mon.	Tue.	Wed.	Thu.	Fri.	Sat.	Sun.
Milk bottles ordered	12	15	9	10	12	4	2

8

Month	J	F	M	A	M	J	J	A	S	O	N	D
Arrests	64	47	42	38	37	44	48	51	45	39	49	58

Exercise 71B

Draw a line graph for each of the following tables.

1

Day	Mon.	Tue.	Wed.	Thu.	Fri.
Detentions	5	8	4	7	10

2

Week	1	2	3	4	5	6
Overtime (hours)	4	6	5	$6\frac{1}{2}$	8	4

3

Time	9 a.m.	10 a.m.	11 a.m.	noon	1 p.m.	2 p.m.	3 p.m.	4 p.m.
People in queue	8	9	12	15	14	16	11	7

4

Month	Sep.	Oct.	Nov.	Dec.	Jan.	Feb.	Mar.	Apr.
Highest temperature (°C)	22	19	17	13	9	11	14	18

5

Car reg. letter	E	F	G	H	J	K	L	M	N	P
Miles travelled (1000s)	60	55	50	42	35	33	25	17	11	6

6	Week	1	2	3	4	5	6	7	8
	Appointments	14	23	21	18	9	16	24	19

7	Time (s)	5	10	15	20	25	30	35	40
	Temperature (°C)	25	31	37	45	55	67	71	87

8	Day	Mon.	Tue.	Wed.	Thu.	Fri.	Sat.	Sun.
	Visitors	350	288	307	336	344	380	372

72/ GROUPING DATA

There are some occasions when it is helpful to group data together.

EXAMPLE

▶ Group this data together in a frequency table.

66   69   75   63   34   80   75   33   88   59   38
97   72   31   77   27   47   68   78   72   74   19
85   48   22   93   43   48   58   50

Mark	Tally	Frequency
0–9		0
10–19	I	1
20–29	II	2
30–39	IIII	4
40–49	IIII	4
50–59	III	3
60–69	IIII	4
70–79	⊮ II	7
80–89	III	3
90–99	II	2
	TOTAL	30

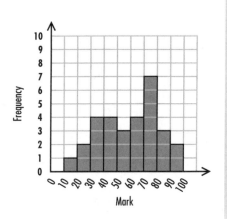

The groups 0–9, 10–19, etc. are called **class intervals**.

The table is called a **frequency table**.

The frequency table can also be shown as a bar chart, which is called a **frequency diagram**.

Exercise 72A

For each set of data (a) draw and complete a frequency table (b) draw a frequency diagram.

1 Number of animals counted in farm buildings.

49	11	30	4	51	43	12	32	20	55	7	43	14	29	35
25	47	36	28	58	32	14	38	63	22	57	33	65	22	18
38	45	9	48	27										

Use class intervals 0–9, 10–19, etc.

2 Number of deliveries made.

20	29	3	10	38	18	26	26	5	31	53	19	43	12	35
24	55	17	57	28	40	12	61	21	43	7	37	47	16	64
24	33	28	8	49										

Use class intervals 0–9, 10–19, etc.

3 Defects recorded in each batch of parts.

16	10	1	21	11	3	15	12	4	23	7	13	19	0	9
25	13	5	27	7	18	30	8	26	0	19	14	6	24	11

Use class intervals 0–4, 5–9, etc.

4 Living relatives of a group of people surveyed.

10	25	5	18	3	20	13	12	26	7	19	13	8	21	12
17	15	9	23	6	14	25	7	19	29	11	23	4	17	14

Use class intervals 0–4, 5–9, etc.

5 Customers served over a period of time.

13	18	3	17	10	15	17	5	14	13	19	7	20	10	14
12	17	18	18	11	20	6	16	16	17	9	14	21	4	23
11	15	13	7	16										

Use class intervals 0–4, 5–9, etc.

6 Number of cars using a car-park at certain times.

255	101	247	153	203	305	41	214	261	172	233	132	195	243	235
160	342	181	183	240	331	53	222	263	127	286	167	232	283	155
279	87	249	212	241	139	177	355	163	294	209	268	144	190	239

Use class intervals 0–49, 50–99, etc.

7 Money recorded.

£7.05	£25.11	£8.99	£31.59	£48.56	£11.21	£45.53	£15.03	£58.50	£34.15	£19.03
£36.21	£37.03	£42.61	£17.83	£26.71	£35.70	£41.63	£12.13	£53.84	£27.41	£47.08
£24.88	£49.32	£47.63	£14.86	£43.64	£48.95	£16.41	£55.12	£30.05	£28.92	£18.63
£42.35	£30.27									

Use class intervals £0.00–£9.99, £10.00–£19.99, etc.

8 Attendances at a series of meetings.

102	130	151	76	143	23	108	126	147	135	118	161	123	129	132
169	28	144	171	127	153	81	40	103	158	92	135	166	178	109
173	63	181	122	129	195	133	155	155	124					

Use class intervals 0–24, 25–49, etc.

9 Speed of typists in words per minute (w.p.m.).

55	70	30	51	25	57	48	53	72	38	43	65	50	54	56
41	55	61	52	63	57	67	58	28	75	35	56	46	46	66
68	45	36	64	83	44	53	76	54	50	79	55	39	61	44

Use class intervals 21–30, 31–40, etc.

10 Money raised for charity.

£144.12	£14.31	£92.11	£180.23	£88.36	£220.41	£41.40	£155.79	£131.28	£50.06
£161.09	£64.51	£121.63	£52.14	£145.69	£166.35	£125.50	£69.71	£189.50	£97.88
£115.10	£43.48	£148.70	£153.82	£29.74	£170.05	£60.15	£89.42	£74.20	£194.97
£150.22	£57.30	£80.90	£123.67	£45.73	£96.92	£107.96	£46.41	£139.23	£205.74
£80.64	£133.65	£173.90	£61.32	£151.50					

Use class intervals £0.00–£39.99, £40.00–£79.99, etc.

Exercise 72B

For each set of data (a) draw and complete a frequency table (b) draw a frequency diagram.

1 Children killed on the roads.

3	9	1	6	4	10	7	5	9	2	8	8	4	5	8
6	5	7	7	3	9	4	6	5	1	10	4	6	7	4
8	5	2	6	7	3	5	6	9	7					

Use class intervals 1–2, 3–4, etc.

2 Test marks for 30 pupils.

| 40 | 59 | 30 | 53 | 8 | 51 | 39 | 17 | 56 | 36 | 24 | 43 | 35 | 47 | 47 |
| 51 | 49 | 12 | 61 | 41 | 21 | 63 | 34 | 59 | 28 | 50 | 50 | 39 | 57 | 48 |

Use class intervals 0–9, 10–19, etc.

3 Amounts of money spent.

£2.04	£0.20	£1.15	£3.51	£2.50	£0.64	£2.75	£1.32	£2.59	£2.84	£0.55
£1.46	£2.61	£4.49	£1.36	£3.62	£2.40	£0.32	£2.19	£2.66	£1.21	£1.72
£5.07	£2.78	£4.35	£2.24	£0.47	£1.99	£2.28	£1.50	£0.81	£1.94	

Use class intervals £0–£0.99, £1.00–£1.99, etc.

4 IQ scores.

105	111	92	101	106	84	114	102	106	96	115	98	112	97	107
104	93	98	87	117	103	118	89	102	107	108	90	109	104	100
105	95													

Use class intervals 81–85, 86–90, etc.

5 Points scored in a competition.

| 20 | 10 | 16 | 24 | 2 | 22 | 13 | 3 | 15 | 18 | 6 | 11 | 23 | 23 | 9 | 19 | 26 |
| 18 | 25 | 14 | 17 | 23 | 11 | 26 | 21 | 4 | 24 | 19 | 7 | 13 | 16 | 12 | 5 | |

Use class intervals 0–4, 5–9, etc.

6 Annual income recorded.

£14111	£9150	£16964	£12215	£23737	£3581	£17062	£8617	£10325	£14759
£16735	£4526	£13021	£16620	£5524	£12553	£7002	£18245	£7627	£13283
£8435	£19545	£14309	£8442	£21541	£18915	£6847	£9003	£15074	£21391
£14077	£7870	£11994	£17472	£13039	£15000				

Use class intervals £0–£3999, £4000–£7999, etc.

7 Speed of typists, in words per minute (w.p.m.).

76	28	51	71	64	38	62	52	68	72	71	42	85	45	71
53	49	65	53	58	76	55	59	61	72	25	74	81	67	75
61	80	62	55	67	57	74	87	78	88

Use class intervals 21–30, 31–40, etc.

8 The number of tins in each batch.

560	605	505	570	445	520	655	660	525	610	710	465	730	620	675
700	535	645	625	545	520	620	575	590	530	625	470	670	525	640
610	680	480	740	580	625	630	570	580	675	540	625	690	540	575

Use class intervals 400–449, 450–499, etc.

9 Number of items in each delivery.

145	235	25	123	165	85	125	190	90	165	94	140	230	98	163
218	100	42	170	85	270	37	134	75	83	250	51	180	31	115
65	250	130	118	150	186	100	73	215	63	184	125	150	41	164
90	200	180	89	225

Use class intervals 0–40, 41–80, etc.

10 Pupil marks (%).

70	11	51	90	80	19	60	73	45	74	50	69	51	93	78
20	67	85	44	53	66	53	75	74	65	30	55	79	40	50
72	58	34	65	75	55	73	55	82	38	58	80	25	88	48
70	57	85	49	60

Use class intervals 10–19, 20–29, etc.

73/ INTERPRETING PIE CHARTS

Exercise 73A

Use the information shown in each pie chart to answer the questions.

1

Uses of energy in the home.

(a) For which purpose is the most energy used?

(b) How many times more energy is used on heating compared with hot water?

2

Accommodation used.

(a) Which type of accommodation was most popular?

(b) Which type of accommodation was least popular?

(c) One hundred people were questioned. How many were accommodated in a flat?

(d) Which two types of accommodation were equally popular?

3

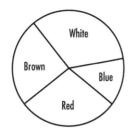

Four most popular colours of cars.

(a) Which colour was the most popular?

(b) Which colour was the third most popular?

(c) Which colour represents a quarter of the pie chart?

4

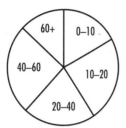

Age distribution of the population (in years).

(a) Estimate the size of the age group (i) 0–10 (ii) 40–60 as a fraction of the population.

(b) Which is the smallest sector in the pie chart?

(c) Which two groups are the same size?

5

Holiday destination.

(a) Which is the most popular holiday destination?

(b) Which is the least popular holiday destination?

(c) Which two parts of the world have the same popularity?

6

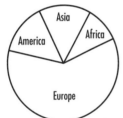

Export destinations for a company (by value of goods).

(a) Which destination receives the greatest value of goods?

(b) To which two places are the same value of goods exported?

(c) If exports to Asia are valued at £5m, estimate the value of exports to Europe.

7

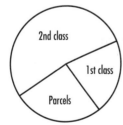

Money spent on postage.

(a) What fraction of the money was spent on parcels?

(b) What was the least amount of money spent on?

(c) What was the most amount of money spent on?

8

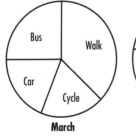

March   June

Transport to school.

(a) Which method of transport was used less in June?

(b) Which method of transport was used more in June?

(c) Which was the least popular method of transport in June?

(d) What fraction of the pupils used the bus in March?

Exercise 73B

Use the information shown in each pie chart to answer the questions.

1

Homework received.

(a) Which subject had the most homework?

(b) Which subject had the least homework?

(c) Which subject had half as much homework as Maths?

2

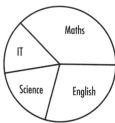

Uses of computers in the home.

(a) For which purpose are computers used the most?

(b) For which purpose are computers used the least?

(c) What fraction of the total use is 'educational'?

3

Pets.

(a) Which pet is the most popular?

(b) Forty people were questioned. How many had (i) a cat (ii) mice?

(c) Which two pets were equally popular?

4

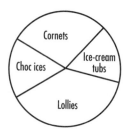

Choices of ice cream.

(a) Which two types of ice cream are equally popular?

(b) What is the most popular type of ice cream sold?

(c) What fraction of the total sales is 'lollies'?

5

Favourite sports.

(a) Which is the least favourite sport?

(b) Which sector represents one-fifth of the pie chart?

(c) Which sport is half as popular as football?

6

Results in an examination.

(a) Which type of result was awarded the most?

(b) Which type of result was awarded the least?

(c) Results were awarded to 100 students. How many received a result of 'distinction'?

7

Time spent in school.

(a) Which activity had least time spent on it?

(b) Which activity had most time spent on it?

8

Week 1

Week 1

Sales of crisps.

(a) Which flavours sold less well in the second week?

(b) Which flavour sold better in the second week?

(c) Which flavour was most popular in (i) the first week (ii) the second week?

REVISION

Exercise G

1 Draw a bar line graph to represent the information in the table, which shows the number of pupils absent from a class during one week.

Day	Mon.	Tue.	Wed.	Thu.	Fri.
Pupils absent	6	4	3	5	8

2 Draw a bar chart to represent the information in the table, which shows the number of items sold in a shop by the sales assistants.

Assistant	Denise	Simon	Usman	Tina	Tony
Items sold	23	18	26	21	17

3 Draw a line graph to represent the information in the table, which shows the change in temperature over a period of time.

Time	8 a.m.	10 a.m.	noon	2 p.m.	4 p.m.	6 p.m.
Temperature (°F)	52	55	60	64	61	54

4 Draw a frequency table *and* a diagram to summarise this data which represents points awarded in a competition.

10	15	5	14	20	24	16	8	20	11	17	27	1	29	23
7	14	15	18	13	25	21	12	7	14	29	3	17	12	9
13	22	15	14	6	22	10	4	19	13

Use class intervals 0–4, 5–9, etc.

5 Draw a frequency table *and* a diagram to summarise this data, which represents average percentage marks.

30.1	51.0	4.1	53.5	25.8	32.8	11.4	38.4	21.4	28.0	40.1	22.5	18.0	56.9	17.8
35.0	29.9	39.5	8.3	31.7	10.2	44.5	34.1	13.9	46.2	24.2	6.6	47.6	30.5	15.3
26.5	36.0	9.7	20.3	15.6	28.6	38.4	22.3	49.7	31.2

Use class intervals 0–9.99, 10–19.9, etc.

Exercise GG

1 The graph shows the rise and fall in the value of a portfolio of shares, over a two-week period.

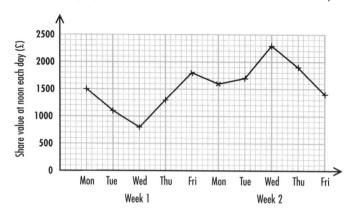

(a) What was the lowest value of the shares?

(b) What was the highest value of the shares?

(c) On which days was the value
(i) £1300 (ii) £1600 (iii) £1900?

(d) What was the value of the shares on
(i) Tuesday Week 1 (ii) Friday Week 1
(iii) Tuesday Week 2?

(e) By how much did the value of the shares change (i) during Week 1
(ii) during Week 2
(iii) over the full two-week period?

2 The graph shows the temperature of water as it is heated.

(a) What is the temperature after
(i) 30 s (ii) 50 s (iii) 80 s?

(b) How long does it take for the temperature to reach (i) 55°C
(ii) 60°C (iii) 30°C?

(c) By how much does the temperature increase between (i) 20 s and 40 s
(ii) 60 s and 80 s?

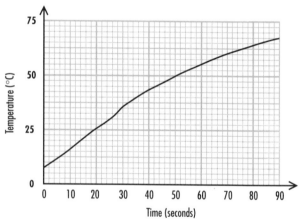

3 The number of passengers in a fleet of minibuses is recorded.

17	10	26	4	20	15	13	6	22	11	24	16	25	20	22	15
11	22	24	19	23	14	26	19	21	27	8	17	16	14	18	4
18	23	16	26	12	28	23	12	28	21	25	9	24	29		

(a) Draw a frequency table and diagram to summarise this data.
Use class intervals 0–4, 5–9, etc.
(b) For which class interval were there the most passengers?
(c) How many minibuses carried less than 10 passengers?
(d) How many minibuses carried more than 19 passengers?
(e) How many minibuses were there altogether?

4

The pie chart shows sugar sales of four types of sugar.

(a) Which types of sugar had about equal sales?

(b) Which type of sugar was sold the least?

(c) How many times more granulated sugar was sold than brown sugar?

Two easily found averages are the mode and the median.
The **mode** is the value which occurs the most.
The **median** is the value which is *strictly* in the middle of the list when it is written in order of size.

EXAMPLE

▶ Find (a) the mode and (b) the median of these numbers.

5	2	9	6	3	10	4	6	2	8	9	7	3
5	12	8	2	11	10	6	9	7	6	12	7	

First write the list in numerical order:

2 2 2 3 3 4 5 5 6 6 6 6 7 7 7 8 8 9 9 9 10 10 11 12 12
                              ↑ middle number

(a) The mode is the number 6, because there are more 6s than any other number.

(b) There are 25 numbers. The middle number is the 13th one in the list.
    So the median is the number 7.

When there is an even number, there is no strict middle value, and the median is the number in-between the middle *two* numbers, for example:

2 2 3 3 4 4 5 5 6 6 7 7
        ↑ the middle value = 4.5 or $4\frac{1}{2}$

Exercise 74A

For each set of numbers find (a) the mode (b) the median.

1   1, 1, 2, 3, 4, 4, 5, 5, 5, 6, 6

2   2, 3, 3, 3, 4, 4, 5, 5, 6, 7, 7, 8

3   0, 0, 1, 2, 3, 3, 4, 5, 5, 5, 6, 7, 7

4   12, 14, 14, 15, 17, 17, 17, 18, 19, 19, 20, 21, 21, 22

5   3, 4, 6, 2, 1, 2, 3, 5, 2, 5

6   10, 13, 7, 10, 3, 6, 15, 14, 11, 6, 9, 10, 15, 5, 11

7   74, 81, 67, 85, 64, 75, 77, 60, 81, 73, 86, 81, 75, 70, 67

8   56, 78, 80, 21, 10, 42, 8, 56, 72, 30, 21, 60, 78, 21

9   31, 35, 36, 33, 32, 35, 36, 31, 34, 33, 36, 34, 32, 32, 36, 34

10 Minutes taken to do a test.
      15, 18, 9, 10, 10, 12, 8, 9, 12, 16, 13, 8, 11, 9, 14, 15

11 Number of people in a lift.
      3, 6, 7, 1, 4, 5, 7, 5, 10, 5, 7, 8, 1, 2, 10, 1, 4, 2, 4, 4, 6, 8

12 Raffle tickets bought.
      2, 9, 1, 4, 10, 2, 6, 3, 1, 7, 10, 5, 2, 5, 8, 8, 7

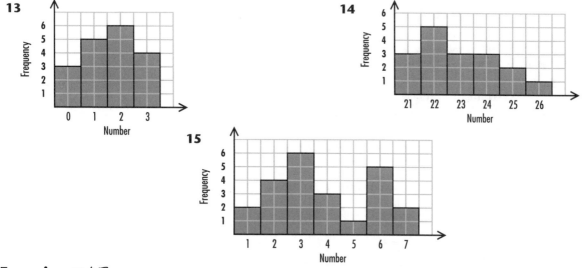

Exercise 74B

For each set of numbers find (a) the mode (b) the median.

1 1, 1, 2, 2, 2, 3, 4, 4, 5, 6, 6,

2 0, 0, 1, 2, 4, 4, 5, 6, 7, 7, 7, 8, 8, 9

3 8, 9, 10, 10, 11, 11, 11, 12, 13, 13, 14, 15, 16, 16, 17

4 22, 25, 26, 26, 28, 30, 31, 34, 35, 35, 35, 37, 38

5 7, 2, 4, 1, 6, 5, 8, 1, 3, 6, 4, 7, 6

6 3, 12, 10, 14, 11, 9, 4, 3, 6, 2, 5, 7, 13, 9, 5, 3, 12

7 19, 23, 21, 27, 25, 25, 18, 22, 20, 27, 25, 26, 22, 24, 19, 23

8 58, 55, 52, 53, 59, 56, 54, 57, 53, 51, 50, 54, 51, 50, 50, 56, 58

9 5, 0, 1, 6, 6, 5, 7, 4, 2, 0, 1, 5, 3, 4, 2, 5, 7, 3, 0, 3, 6

10 Points awarded in a competition.
9, 7, 8, 11, 12, 9, 5, 8, 7, 10, 12, 8, 5, 10, 9, 12, 11, 5, 8

11 Test marks out of 30.
20, 21, 25, 22, 22, 17, 13, 21, 23, 15, 9, 10, 22, 23, 20

12 Time taken to run a cross-country course (minutes)
44, 39, 38, 45, 46, 41, 35, 32, 38, 44, 48, 45, 43, 34, 40, 40, 45

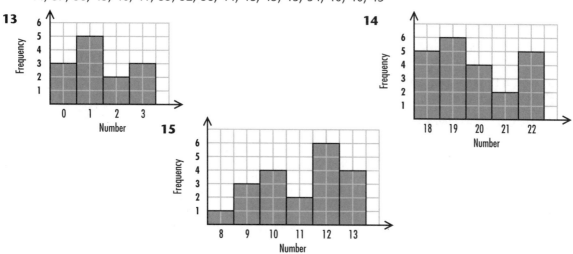

The **mean** is a type of average.

$$\text{Mean} = \frac{\text{sum of all the numbers}}{\text{how many numbers there are}}$$

The **range** tells us how widely spread the numbers are.

Range = largest number – smallest number

> **EXAMPLE**
>
> ▶ Find the mean and range of 3, 7, 9, 10, 12, 14, 15, 17, 20, 22.
>
> $$\text{Mean} = \frac{3+7+9+10+12+14+15+17+20+22}{10} = \frac{129}{10} = 12.9$$
>
> Range = 22 – 3 = 19
>
> Note: The range is a single number.

Exercise 75A

For each set of numbers find (a) the mean (b) the range.

1 4, 0, 2, 9, 0

2 1, 1, 2, 2, 4, 5, 5, 0

3 21, 12, 18, 15, 9

4 62, 61, 63, 62

5 2, 2, 2, 3, 4, 5

6 143, 205, 54, 48, 56

7 2, 2, 1, 5, 5, 6, 1, 4, 3, 9

8 14, 12, 16, 26, 24, 18, 22, 14, 16

9 3, 17, 26, 24, 12, 17, 32, 14, 25, 2

10 8, 7, 8, 6, 7, 6, 1, 8, 7, 9

11 3, 1, 2, 4, 2, 1, 2, 2, 3, 3

12 1, 3, 2, 3, 1, 2, 1, 3, 1, 4

13 36, 38, 42, 39, 40, 42, 43, 36

14 74, 63, 65, 72, 73, 69, 66, 80

15 4, 2, 6, 3, 3, 5, 4, 9, 2, 10, 3, 4, 3, 4, 7

16 14, 14, 19, 15, 17, 11, 16, 16, 13

17 16, 43, 28, 26, 26, 35, 28, 34, 28, 37

18 50, 30, 90, 30, 130, 70, 60, 100, 80, 40

19 67, 55, 57, 15, 82, 78, 12, 10, 58, 90

20 17, 45, 86, 62, 80, 48, 41, 31, 51, 99

Exercise 75B

For each set of numbers find (a) the mean (b) the range.

1 3, 2, 4, 2, 0, 1

2 5, 4, 3, 2, 3, 7

3 1, 1, 2, 2, 3, 4, 4, 4, 6

4 7, 0, 5, 5, 4, 3

5 108, 119, 132, 147, 103

6 5, 12, 15, 17, 14

7 9, 5, 10, 7, 9, 5, 9, 10, 2, 3

8 8, 5, 8, 15, 15, 10, 9, 12, 9, 8, 6, 3

9 76, 67, 69, 81, 69, 73, 67, 84

10 34, 28, 35, 26, 26, 28, 43, 16

11 1, 2, 4, 3, 1, 4, 1, 2, 3, 0

12 79, 73, 69, 70, 72, 75, 68, 72

13 39, 42, 41, 37, 44, 42, 39, 38

14 47, 31, 86, 25, 125, 75, 64, 95, 84, 37

15 3, 4, 5, 8, 6, 8, 9, 6, 7, 6, 8, 6, 4, 4

16 12, 8, 14, 27, 28, 39, 35, 29, 19, 23, 18, 6

17 60, 90, 50, 30, 70, 50, 140, 80, 70, 40

18 20, 140, 90, 60, 220, 490, 30, 90, 110, 370

19 20, 135, 85, 65, 220, 565, 25, 85, 105, 183

20 65, 90, 45, 30, 75, 50, 140, 85, 70, 45

EXAMPLE

▶ The average cost of 8 pens was 53p. What was the total cost of the pens?

The total cost is 8×53 p = £4.24.

EXAMPLE

▶ The number of minutes customers queue at the tills at two supermarkets is recorded:

Low Price: 3 2 4 6 7 5 4 5 8 7 4 5
Budget: 2 3 6 5 4 7 8 8 7 6

Which supermarket had the least mean waiting time?

The mean for Low Price is: $60 \div 12 = 5$ minutes
The mean for Budget is: $56 \div 10 = 5.6$ minutes
Low Price had the least mean waiting time.

Exercise 76A

1 The mean of six numbers is 5. What is the total of the six numbers?

2 The mean price of four books was £6.80 What is the total cost of the four books?

3 John's mean mark over five tests is 63%. Find his total mark.

4 The average of twelve number is 7. What is the total of the twelve numbers?

5 The range of five numbers is 4. Four of the numbers are 4, 5, 6, 7. The smallest number is missing. What is the fifth number?

6 The range of seven numbers is 13. Six of the numbers are 4, 5, 7, 8, 10, 14. The smallest number is missing. What is it?.

7 The range of eight numbers is 6. Seven of the numbers are 6, 7, 7, 9, 9, 10, 11. The smallest number is missing. Find the smallest number.

8 The time taken for two typists to complete each of a number of documents is listed below.

Valerie   4 6 8 5 7 10 9 4 5 5 6 7
Shamsa   8 7 8 8 4 5 3 8 9 7 6

Who was the quicker typist?

9 The attendances in two classes were recorded:

Class TR 28 27 29 28 30 30 24 24 25 25
Class BH 26 26 21 21 25 25 25 25 28 28

Which class had the best attendance?

10 The number of passengers carried by two ferries is as follows:

Blue Line   486 467 443 428 479 410 387
Neptune   394 461 420 475 523 458 532 535 487

Which ferry carried more passengers on average per trip?

11 The marks obtained by boys and girls in a class are compared:

Boys   65 56 35 46 89 56 76 58 72 65 54 38 72
Girls   68 38 52 75 79 55 48 64 28 85 43

Did boys or girls score better marks?

12 These are the goals scored by two hockey teams:

Revellers	3	4	1	0	2	1	2	0	5	3
Tigers	4	0	0	4	2	2	3	2		

Which team had a better standard of play?

13 Listed below are the test marks achieved by two students.

Dipak	75	85	75	50	32	66		
Serafim	35	50	70	65	85	66	83	60

Who has achieved the better marks?

14 Two competitors in a competition list their marks.

Jenny	20	21	14	15	17	18	20	15	20	15
Susan	18	13	22	23	20	16	14	21	14	21

Who is the better competitor?

15 Two ladies list the maximum weight they each lift on several visits to a gym (in kg).

Lynn	60	66	50	55	63	64	64	60
Belinda	54	61	58	65	63	60		

Who is the better weight-lifter?

Exercise 76B

1 The mean of eight numbers is 9. What is the total of the eight numbers?

2 The mean weight of twelve tools is 1.3 kg. What is the total weight of all twelve tools?

3 Jill's mean mark over seven tests is 68%. Find her total mark.

4 The mean of nine numbers is 12. What is the total of the nine numbers?

5 The range of seven numbers is 2. Six of the numbers are 4, 4, 4, 5, 5, 5. The largest number is missing. Find this number.

6 The range of six numbers is 6. Five of the numbers are 3, 4, 5, 7, 8. The largest number is missing. Find this number.

7 The range of eight numbers is 9. Seven of the numbers are 3, 5, 6, 7, 8, 10, 11. The smallest number is missing. What is this number?

8 Two groups of pupils were awarded marks for work done:

Group A	10	13	21	14	20	13	20
Group B	10	12	14	16	11	15	

Which group had the higher mean marks?

9 The time taken, in seconds, for a range of electronic parts to be assembled by two workers is listed below.

Sam	12	13	9	14	16	15	12	9	12	12	13	15		
Pat	10	16	9	12	10	9	15	14	9	10	12	8	14	12

Which worker completed the assemblies in the quicker time?

10 The heights, in centimetres, of the grandchildren in two families were recorded:

Smiths	162	142	156	134	145	140	136		
Browns	170	148	143	158	150	135	157	141	147	151

Which family had the taller children?

11 The ages of people, in years, attending two pensioner's club are recorded.

Crest Club	86	64	79	58	72	69	60	75	65	82	70
Third Age Club	80	65	70	76	60	64	75	62			

Which club has the older pensioners?

12 The number of items sold by two salesmen over a period of days is shown below.

Ben   14   15   17   14   13   15   16   18   19   19   15   16
Daniel   16   13   12   14   12   15   12   13   12   11

Which salesman had sold the larger number of items per day?

13 The daytime temperatures, in °F, were recorded at two resorts.

Blackpool   80   84   88   81   79   84   82   78   88   90   87
Scarborough   78   81   85   83   88   81   84   87   82

Which resort had the higher temperatures.

14 The number of records sold in each of two shops is recorded.

Disco Records   23   12   18   17   24   20   21   23   20   18   19
Hard Hits   20   17   18   21   19   20   20   23   19   20

Which shop appears to be better at selling records?

15 The points scored by two competitors is shown below.

June   8   9   4   8   7   6   4   5   9   8   7   6
Sally   6   8   7   9   8   8   6   7   5   7

Which competitor has the higher mean marks?

77/ PROBABILITY SCALE

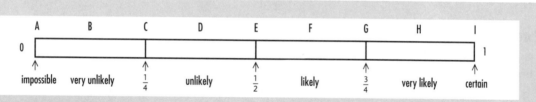

This is a **probability scale**.

The probability of an event happening can be shown as a position on the scale.

'Evens' is a term which is used to describe events which are equally likely to happen. This is normally indicated by the midpoint position in the table.

> **EXAMPLES**
>
> ▶ Events which will never happen (impossible) are shown at position A.
> Events which will certainly happen are shown at position I.
> Events which might happen once in every four events, on average, are shown at position C.
> Events which are unlikely, but might happen more than once in every four events on average, are shown at position D.
>
> The probability of a student receiving homework on a particular night is 'likely', which can be shown at position F on the probability scale.

Exercise 77A

For each statement below write down the letter of the position on the probability scale at which it could be shown.

1 A coin is tossed and lands showing 'heads'.

2 A hundred people fit into a car.

3 You throw a number less than 4 on a dice.

4 It will not rain between 4 a.m. and 9 a.m.

5 The sun will rise in the morning.

6 A watch stops between 7 and 9.

7 You throw a 3 with a dice.

8 The driver of a car containing three ladies and one man is female.

9 A red pen is picked from a bag containing five red pens and three blue pens.

10 Concorde can circle the earth in 80 minutes.

11 A light switch is found switched on.

12 You throw a number less than 7 with a dice.

13 When you turn the TV on, the adverts are *not* being shown.

14 A traffic light is on red.

15 The first ten pupils who arrive at the school are either male or female.

16 You throw a number less than 4 on an octagonal dice.

17 It will not rain for 12 months.

18 The second hand of a stopwatch will stop between 0 and 45 seconds.

19 Picking a pupil at random and finding the pupil is female.

20 There will be no road accidents in the country in a day.

Exercise 77B

For each statement below write down the letter of the position on the probability scale at which it could be shown.

1 A baby born is a girl.

2 A coin is tossed and lands showing either 'heads' or 'tails'.

3 One corner of a square is selected at random.

4 You throw two dice and get the number 13.

5 An animal picked from three mice and a hamster will be a mouse.

6 Throwing an odd number on a dice.

7 A coin that is slightly biased in favour of 'heads' is thrown to show a 'head'.

8 A man riding a bicycle overtakes a plane taking off.

9 Prices will increase this year.

10 A stopwatch times a minute as 60 seconds.

11 A blue card is selected from a box containing three blue, three red and two green cards.

12 It will not rain between 4 a.m. and 10 a.m.

13 The number 7 is thrown on an octagonal dice.

14 A watch stops between 2 and 4.

15 A man runs a mile in two minutes.

16 Throwing the numbers 1, 2, 3 or 4 on a dice.

17 Picking a day at random and finding it is a dry day rather than a wet day.

18 A man walks 30 miles in a straight line and crosses at least one road.

19 When you turn the TV on, it is showing a News programme.

20 There will be snow this winter.

78/ OUTCOMES

When an event happens, the **outcomes** are what might occur.

EXAMPLE
▶

Two coins are thrown together. All the possible outcomes are:

Head Head   Head Tail   Tail Head   Tail Tail

Exercise 78A

For each situation write out a list of all the possible outcomes.

1 Picking a vowel from the letters of the alphabet.

2 Throwing two dice together.

3 Throwing a single coin.

4 Throwing an octagonal dice.

5 Picking a letter from the word MATHEMATICS.

6 Throwing this spinner.

7 Throwing this spinner and a coin together.

8 Throwing these spinners together.

          9 Throwing these spinners together.

10 Throwing four coins together.

11 Throwing these spinners together.

12 Picking any two cards from those shown.

13 Picking three beads from a bag containing ten red, ten green and ten blue beads.

| BLUE | RED | GREEN | YELLOW |
| BLUE | RED | GREEN | YELLOW |

Exercise 78B

For each situation write out a list of all the possible outcomes.

1 Picking a letter from the last five letters in the alphabet.

2 Throwing a single dice.

3 Throwing three coins together.

4 Picking an even number from the face of a 24-hour clock.

5 Picking an odd number from all the numbers less than 12.

6 Picking a letter from the word MISSISSIPPI.

7 Throwing this spinner and a coin together.

8 Throwing this spinner.

9 Choosing any two countries from England, Wales, Scotland and Northern Ireland.

10 Throwing an octagonal dice and a coin together.

11 Picking any three cards from those shown.

| BLUE | RED | GREEN | YELLOW |
| BLUE | RED | GREEN | YELLOW |

12 Picking three beads from a bag containing ten yellow, ten white and ten pink beads.

13 Picking three beads from a bag containing ten black and ten white beads.

79/ PROBABILITY FRACTIONS

Probabilities can be expressed as fractions, decimals or percentages.
Measures of probability are normally given as fractions between 0 and 1.

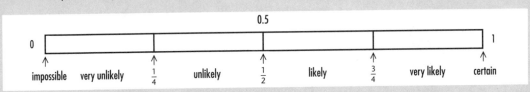

If an event definitely will not happen it has a probability of 0.
If an event definitely **will** happen it has a probability of 1.
If two events are equally likely to happen then it is 'evens' that either event will happen, and the probability of each event happening is $\frac{1}{2}$.

EXAMPLE

► In a box are five beads: A, B, C, D, E. If each one is equally likely to be picked out, write down the probability that bead D will be randomly selected.

Number of possible outcomes (A, B, C, D or E) = 5

Probability of one event (bead D) = $\frac{1}{5}$ or 0.2 or 20%

EXAMPLE

► Write down the probability of throwing the number 5 with a dice.

Number of possible outcomes (1, 2, 3, 4, 5 or 6) = 6

Probability of one event (a 5) = $\frac{1}{6}$

Exercise 79A

In each case all outcomes can be assumed to be equally likely. Write down the probability of each of the following events happening.

1 Throwing the number 6 on a dice.

2 Throwing a coin and getting 'heads'.

3 Picking the number 7 from the numbers 1 to 10.

4 Selecting the letter T from the word JUSTICE.

5 Picking the number 4 from the numbers 3, 4, 5, 6, 7.

6 Picking March from a list of months on a calendar.

7 Winning first prize in a 250-ticket raffle after having bought one ticket.

8 Picking an odd number from the list:
2, 6, 10, 13, 14, 18, 24

9 Throwing the letter E on the spinner.

10 Picking a red ball from a bag containing a red, a blue, and a green ball.

11 Throwing the number 3 with a dice.

12 Picking the number 341 from these cards.

205 341 432 102

217 512 415 204

13 Selecting the number 3 from the first seven odd numbers.

14 Throwing the number 7 on this spinner.

15 Winning first prize in a 1000-ticket lottery after having bought one ticket.

16 Guessing the exact day in December on which a friend was born.

17 Picking the one bad egg in a carton of six.

18 Selecting the jar which contains honey.

19 Selecting the main news channel from 28 channels on the satellite system.

20 Picking the salt pot.

Exercise 79B

In each case all outcomes can be assumed to be equally likely. Write down the probability of each of the following events happening.

1 Throwing a coin and getting 'tails'.

2 Picking Friday from a list of days on a calendar.

3 Getting first prize in a 200-ticket raffle after having bought one ticket.

4 Picking the number 12 from the number 1 to 20.

5 Throwing the number 2 with a dice.

6 Picking the number 6 from the numbers on a clock face.

7 Throwing the letter D on this spinner.

8 Selecting a red pen from a box containing a red pen and a blue pen.

9 Picking an even number from the list:
13, 7, 5, 9, 6, 11, 15, 19.

10 Throwing the number 2 on this spinner.

11 Selecting the number 8 from the first six even numbers.

12 Picking the number 531 from these cards.

13 Throwing the number 4 with a dice.

14 Winning first prize in a 5000-ticket lottery after having bought one ticket.

15 Selecting the ITV channel from the five channels on a television.

16 The needle spinning and stopping on RED.

17 Guessing the exact day in April on which a friend was born.

18 Picking the one bad apple in a box of 20 apples.

19 Selecting the quietest student from a class of 30.

20 Picking the correct book from this pile of books.

REVISION

Exercise H

1 For each set of numbers find (i) the median (ii) the mean (iii) the range.

(a) 3   5   5   6   7   7   8   8   8   9   9   10   12

(b) 1   1   1   2   2   3   3   3   4   4   4   4   5   5   5

(c) 46   42   43   44   44   41   46   43   42   47   43   45   44   43

(d) 6   0   1   3   4   3   2   7   3   6   0   1   5   2   3   1   4

(e) 22   18   20   19   25   24   23   23   18   20   24   22   20   23   21

(f) 32   15   8   25   35   15   22   12   25   30   18   14   25   28   20

2 The mean of seven numbers is 10. What is the total of the seven numbers?

3 The mean of nine numbers is 8.5. What is the total of the nine numbers?

4 The range of seven numbers is 9. Six of the numbers are 5, 5, 6, 8, 9, 9. The largest number is missing. Find this number.

5 The range of ten numbers is 12. Nine of the numbers are 7, 10, 10, 10, 12, 13, 14, 14, 18. The smallest number is missing. Find this number.

Exercise HH

1 Joanne and Gary each throw a dice for one minute, and record their scores.

Joanne 4   2   6   3   3   6   1   4   2   1   6   3   4   5   5

Gary   5   6   1   2   2   3   6   5   2   3   3   6   5

Who threw the higher mean score?

2 These are the scores achieved by two teams in games they have played:

Hotspurs 8   6   12   0   11   15   12   8   7   4   3   0   5

Rangers   1   10   12   0   8   18   15   9   11   15   4   3

Which team achieved the better results?

3 Two snails are left for a number of periods of five minutes each. The distance they have moved is then measured. This distance, in centimetres, is shown below.

Harold 8   10   15   12   11   2   5   8   6   12   4   5   8

Brian   7   11   9   10   4   15   5   3   8   7   15   6

Which snail was the faster?

4

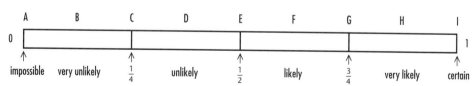

For each statement write down the letter of the position on the probability scale at which it should be shown.

(a) You pick a terrapin from a tank and find it is male.

(b) A dog gives birth to 101 puppies in a day.

(c) You pick a red pen from a bag containing one red pen and three black pens.

(d) The earth will go around the sun in approximately one year.

(e) The letter A is picked from the letters in the word AARDVARC.

5   For each situation write out a list of the possible outcomes.

   (a) Throwing a coin and a dice together.

   (b) Throwing three coins together.

   (c) Throwing these spinners together.

   (d) Throwing these spinners together.

6   In each of these cases all outcomes are assumed to be equally likely. Write down the probability of each of the following events happening.

   (a) Throwing the number 3 with a dice.

   (b) Selecting an even number from the numbers in this list: 1, 3, 5, 7, 8, 9, 13, 17.

   (c) Guessing the exact day in April on which a friend was born.

   (d) Winning first prize in a 700-ticket raffle after having bought one ticket.